Cities in a World Economy

Sociology for a New Century

A PINE FORGE PRESS SERIES

Edited by Charles Ragin, Wendy Griswold, and Larry Griffin

Sociology for a New Century brings the best current scholarship to today's students in a series of short texts authored by leaders of a new generation of social scientists. Each book addresses its subject from a comparative, historical, global perspective, and, in doing so, connects social science to the wider concerns of students seeking to make sense of our dramatically changing world.

- *How Societies Change* Daniel Chirot
- *Culture and Societies in a Changing World* Wendy Griswold
- *Crime and Disrepute* John Hagan
- *Constructing Social Research* Charles C. Ragin
- *Women and Men at Work* Barbara Reskin and Irene Padavic
- *Cities in a World Economy* Saskia Sassen

Forthcoming:
- *Social Psychology and Social Institutions* Denise and William Bielby
- *Global Transitions: Emerging Patterns of Inequality* York Bradshaw and Michael Wallace
- *Schools and Societies* Steven Brint
- *The Social Ecology of Natural Resources and Development* Stephen G. Bunker
- *Ethnic Dynamics in the Modern World* Stephen Cornell
- *The Sociology of Childhood* William A. Corsaro
- *Racism and the Modern World* Wilmot James
- *Gods in the Global Village* Lester Kurtz
- *Waves of Democracy* John Markoff
- *A Global View of Development* Philip McMichael
- *Health and Society* Bernice Pescosolido
- *Organizations in a World Economy* Walter W. Powell

Cities in a World Economy

Saskia Sassen
Columbia University

PINE FORGE PRESS
Thousand Oaks ◆ London ◆ New Delhi

For information, address:

 Pine Forge Press
A Sage Publications Company
2455 Teller Road
Thousand Oaks, California 91320
(805) 499-4224
Internet:sdr@pfp.sagepub.com

Production: Scratchgravel Publishing Services
Designer: Lisa S. Mirski
Typesetter: Scratchgravel Publishing Services
Cover: Lisa S. Mirski
Print Buyer: Anna Chin
Printer: Malloy Lithographing, Inc.

Printed in the United States of America

94 95 96 97 98 10 9 8 7 6 5 4 3 2 1

Library of Congress Cataloging-in-Publication Data

Sassen, Saskia.
    Cities in a world economy / Saskia Sassen.
        p.   cm. — (Sociology for a new century)
    Includes bibliographical references and index.
    ISBN 0-8039-9005-7 (pbk. : alk. paper)
    1. Urban economics. 2. Metropolitan areas—Cross-cultural
studies. 3. Cities and towns—Cross-cultural studies.
4. Sociology, Urban. I. Title. II. Series.
HT321.S28   1994
330.9173'2—dc20   93-47613
                                                                         CIP

We want to thank the following for allowing us to reproduce materials: European Institute of Urban Affairs (Liverpool, John Moores University); the Programme on Transnational Corporations of the United Nations Conference on Trade and Development; *Contemporary Sociology;* Princeton University Press; the Urban Development Division of the World Bank; Belhaven Press.

 This book is printed on acid-free paper that meets Environmental Protection Agency standards for recycled paper

For Hilary, my son

Contents

About the Author / *ix*

Foreword / *xi*

Preface / *xiii*

1 Place and Production in the Global Economy / 1

2 The Urban Impact of Economic Globalization / 9
The Global Economy Today / 10
Strategic Places / 18
Conclusion: After the Pax Americana / 27

3 New Inequalities among Cities / 29
Impacts on Primate Systems: The Case of Latin America and the
    Caribbean / 29
Impacts on Balanced Urban Systems: The Case of Europe / 39
Transnational Urban Systems / 47
Conclusion: Urban Growth and Its Multiple Meanings / 51

**4 The New Urban Economy: The Intersection of Global
    Processes and Place / 53**
Producer Services / 55
The Formation of a New Production Complex / 65
Impact of the Late 1980s Financial Crisis on Global City Functions:
    The Case of New York City / 74
Conclusion: Cities as Post-Industrial Production Sites / 76

5 Issues and Case Studies in the New Urban
   Economy / 77

   The Development of Global City Functions:
       The Case of Miami / 78

   The Growing Density and Specialization of Functions in Financial
       Districts: Toronto / 82

   The Concentration of Functions and Geographic Scale: Sydney / 85

   Globalization and Concentration: The Case of Leading Financial
       Centers / 89

   The Space Economy of the Center / 93

   Conclusion: Concentration and the Redefinition of the Center / 96

6 The New Inequalities within Cities / 99

   Transformations in the Organization of the Labor Process / 100

   The Earnings Distribution in a Service-Dominated Economy / 107

   Conclusion: A Widening Gap / 116

7 A New Geography of Centers and Margins: Summary
   and Implications / 119

   The Locus of the Peripheral / 120

   Contested Space / 121

APPENDIX / 125

References / 137

Glossary/Index / 153

ABOUT THE AUTHOR

Saskia Sassen is Professor of Urban Planning at Columbia University. She is the author of *The Mobility of Labor and Capital: A Study in International Investment and Labor Flow* (Cambridge University Press, 1988) and *The Global City: New York, London, Tokyo* (Princeton University Press, 1991). She has published extensively in professional journals and collections. She is now completing a book on international migration for Fischer Verlag in Germany and has begun work on a five-year project entitled "Governance and Accountability in a World Economy."

ABOUT THE PUBLISHER

Pine Forge Press is a new educational publisher, dedicated to publishing innovative books and software throughout the social sciences. On this and any other of our publications, we welcome your comments, ideas, and suggestions. Please call or write to:

Pine Forge Press
A Sage Publications Company
2455 Teller Road
Thousand Oaks, California 91320
(805) 499-4224
Internet:sdr@pfp.sagepub.com

Foreword

Sociology for a New Century offers the best of current sociological thinking to today's students. The goal of the series is to prepare students, and—in the long run—the informed public, for a world that has changed dramatically in the last three decades and one that continues to astonish.

This goal reflects important changes that have taken place in sociology. The discipline has become broader in orientation, with an ever growing interest in research that is comparative, historical, or transnational in orientation. Sociologists are less focused on "American" society as the pinnacle of human achievement and more sensitive to global processes and trends. They also have become less insulated from surrounding social forces. In the 1970s and 1980s sociologists were so obsessed with constructing a science of society that they saw impenetrability as a sign of success. Today, there is a greater effort to connect sociology to the ongoing concerns and experiences of the informed public.

Each book in this series offers a comparative, historical, transnational, or global perspective in some way, to help broaden students' vision. Students need to be sensitized to diversity in today's world and to the sources of diversity. Knowledge of diversity challenges the limitations of conventional ways of thinking about social life. At the same time, students need to be sensitized to the fact that issues that may seem specifically "American" (for example, the women's movement, an aging population bringing a strained social security and health care system, racial conflict, national chauvinism, and so on) are shared by many other countries. Awareness of commonalities undercuts the tendency to view social issues and questions in narrowly American terms and encourages students to seek out the experiences of others for the lessons they offer. Finally, students also need to be sensitized to phenomena that transcend national boundaries, economies, and politics—trends and processes that are supranational (for example, environmental degradation).

This volume does so in two ways. First, it shows how certain characteristics of our contemporary world economy have led to the emergence of a new phenomenon: global cities. Whereas many urban theorists have suggested that cities were becoming economically obsolete, rendered marginal by global telecommunications and the mobility of people and capital, *Cities in a World Economy* reveals how developments in the past decade suggest otherwise. This book introduces students to the way some cities—New York, Tokyo, London, Sao Paulo, Hong Kong, and Sydney among others—have evolved into transnational market "spaces." These developments give new meaning to such fixtures of urban sociology as the centrality of place and the importance of geography in our social world. Second, this book examines the impact of global processes on the social structure of cities, showing how transformations in the organization of labor, the redistribution of earnings, and the restructuring of consumption are contributing to new hierarchies of inequality, both within and among cities around the world.

Preface

Sociologists have tended to study cities by looking at the ecology of urban forms and the distribution of population and institutional centers or by focusing on people and social groups, lifestyles, and urban problems. These approaches are no longer sufficient. Economic globalization, accompanied by the emergence of a global culture, has profoundly altered the social, economic, and political reality of nation-states, cross-national regions, and—the subject of this book—cities. Through the study of the city as one particular site in which global processes take place, I seek to define new concepts useful to understand the intersection of the global and the local in today's world—and tomorrow's.

It is helpful in this context to recall Janet Abu-Lughod, a leading urban sociologist, who has commented that it is impossible to study the city only from a sociological perspective because it requires an understanding of many other realities. Manuel Castells, another major urban sociologist, has added that it is impossible to study the city only from an urban perspective. These two observations mark an empty space in urban sociology, which I seek to address in this book.

Although there has been an international economic system for a long time and a world economy for many centuries, the current situation is distinct in two respects. On the one hand, we have seen the formation of transnational spaces for economic activity where governments play a minimal role, very different from the role they play in international trade for instance. Examples of such spaces are export processing zones, offshore banking centers, and many of the new global financial markets. On the other hand, these transnational spaces for economic activity are located in national territories and are ruled by sovereign nation-states. There is no such entity as a global economy "out there," in some space that exists outside nation-states. Rather, the location of transnational spaces within national territories defines the current phase of the world economy. This new configuration is increasingly being called a global economy to distinguish it from such earlier formations as the old colonial empires or the international economic system of the immediate post–World War II period, in which governments played a crucial regulatory role in international trade, investment, and financial markets.

Understanding how global processes locate in national territories requires new concepts and research strategies. The global city, drawing on and demanding research practices that negotiate the intersection of macroanalysis and ethnography, is one such new concept. It presumes that global processes, from the formation of global financial markets to the rapid growth of foreign direct investment, can be studied through the particular forms in which they materialize in places.

This book shows how some cities—New York, Tokyo, London, Sao Paulo, Hong Kong, Toronto, Miami, Sydney, among others—have evolved into transnational market "spaces." As such cities have prospered, they have come to have more in common with one another than with regional centers in their own nation-states, many of which have declined in importance. Such developments require all those interested in the fate of cities to rethink traditionally held views of cities as subunits of their nation-states or to reassess the importance of geography in our social world. Moreover, the impact of global processes radically transforms the social structure of cities themselves—altering the organization of labor, the distribution of earnings, the structure of consumption, all of which in turn create new patterns of urban social inequality. In *Cities in a World Economy,* I seek to provide the vocabulary and analytic frames with which students and the general reader can grasp this new world of urban forms.

Acknowledgments

I want to thank several individuals and institutions that made it possible to write this book in a rather brief period of time. The Wissenschaftszentrum in Berlin was a generous and intellectually stimulating home. So was the Institute for Advanced Studies in Vienna, most particularly because of Rainer Baubock and the students in my course. These institutions made all the difference in my 1991–1992 sabbatical year in Europe. The Russell Sage Foundation, where I was a visiting scholar in 1992–1993, is well known for its dedicated support of scholars and their work; I want to thank its staff and, most particularly, Vivian Kauffman for her precise and intelligent assistance. The Department of Political Science and the Faculty of Environmental Studies of York University in Toronto sponsored an international summer institute on the global city that allowed me to work with students from a variety of countries and backgrounds; I am particularly thankful to Roger Keil and Leo Panic. Finally, an invitation from the Woodrow Wilson International Center for Scholars to spend the summer of 1993 in Washington, D.C., provided me with the support to complete this book; I am especially grateful to Blair Ruble, Joseph Tulchin, and the members of the Urban Working Group: Paulo Singer, Richard Sennett, and Wilbur Zelinsky. I want to thank the excellent research assistance of Laura Bosco and Mark Williamson at the Woodrow Wilson Center; and Brian Sahd, Kam Wong, and Luc Nadal at Columbia University. Finally, Wendy Griswold, Charles Ragin, and Larry Griffin—the editors of the series—came up with the timely idea of the series; I am glad they convinced me to join the project.

The largest single debt is to Steve Rutter, founding editor of Pine Forge Press; Chiara Huddleston, associate publisher; Victoria Nelson, editor; and Anne Draus of Scratchgravel Publishing Services. Their help, patience, and—it must be said—relentlessness made this book possible, swimming as it was in a sea of other deadlines.

As always, Richard Sennett and Hilary Koob-Sassen were there.

Cities in a World Economy

1

Place and Production in the Global Economy

As the end of the twentieth century approaches, massive developments in telecommunications and the ascendance of information industries have led analysts and politicians to proclaim the end of cities. Cities, they tell us, should now be obsolete as economic entities. With large-scale relocations of offices and factories to less congested and lower cost areas than central cities, the computerized workplace can be located anywhere: in a clerical "factory" in the Bahamas or in a home in the suburbs. The growth of information industries has made it possible for outputs to be transmitted around the globe instantaneously. And the globalization of economic activity suggests that place—particularly the type of place represented by cities—no longer matters.

This is but a partial account, however. These trends are indeed all taking place, but they represent only half of what is happening. Alongside the well-documented spatial dispersal of economic activities, new forms of territorial centralization of top-level management and control operations have appeared. National and global markets, as well as globally integrated operations, require central places where the work of globalization gets done. Furthermore, information industries require a vast physical infrastructure containing strategic nodes with a hyperconcentration of facilities. Finally, even the most advanced information industries have a production process.

Once this process is brought into the analysis, funny things happen; secretaries are part of it, and so are the cleaners of the buildings where the professionals do their work. An economic configuration very different from that suggested by the concept of **information economy** emerges, whereby we recover the material conditions, production sites, and place-boundedness that are also part of globalization and the information economy. A detailed examination of the activities, firms, markets, and physical infrastructure that are involved in globalization and concentrated in cities allows us to see the actual role played by cities in a global

Note: **Boldface** terms in the text are defined in the Glossary/Index.

economy. Thus when telecommunications were introduced on a large scale in all advanced industries in the 1980s, we saw the central business districts of the leading cities and international business centers of the world—New York, Los Angeles, London, Tokyo, Frankfurt, Sao Paulo, Hong Kong, and Sydney, among others—reach their highest densities ever. This explosion in the numbers of firms locating in the downtowns of major cities during that decade goes against what should have been expected according to models emphasizing territorial dispersal; this is especially true given the high cost of locating in a major downtown area.

If telecommunications has not made cities obsolete, has it at least altered the economic function of cities in a global economy? And if this is so, what does it tell us about the importance of place, of the locale, in an era dominated by the imagery and the language of economic globalization and information flows? Is there a new and strategic role for major cities, a role linked to the formation of a truly global economic system, a role not sufficiently recognized by analysts and policymakers? And could it be that the reason this new and strategic role has not been sufficiently recognized is that economic globalization—what it actually takes to implement global markets and processes—is misunderstood?

The notion of a global economy has become deeply entrenched in political and media circles all over the world. Yet its dominant images—the instantaneous transmission of money around the globe, the information economy, the neutralization of distance through **telematics**—are partial and hence profoundly inadequate representations of what globalization and the rise of information economies actually entail for cities. Missing from this abstract model are the actual material processes, activities, and infrastructures that are central to the implementation of globalization. Both overlooking the spatial dimension of economic globalization and overemphasizing the information dimensions have served to distort the role played by major cities in the current phase of economic globalization.

The last 20 years have seen pronounced changes in the geography, composition, and institutional framework of economic globalization. A world economy has been in existence for several centuries, but it has been reconstituted repeatedly over time. A key starting point for this book is the fact that, in each historical period, the world economy has consisted of a distinct combination of geographic areas, industries, and institutional arrangements. One of the important changes over the last 20 years has been the increase in the mobility of capital at both the national and especially the transnational level. The transnational mobility of capital brings about specific forms of articulation among different geographic areas and transformations in the role played by these areas in the world economy.

This trend in turn produces several types of locations for international transactions, the most familiar of which are **export processing zones** and **offshore banking centers**. One question for us, then, is the extent to which major cities are yet another type of *location* for international transactions, though clearly one at a very high level of complexity.

Increased capital mobility does not only bring about changes in the geographic organization of manufacturing production and in the network of financial markets. Increased capital mobility also generates a demand for types of production needed to ensure the management, control, and servicing of this new organization of manufacturing and finance. These new types of production range from the development of telecommunications to specialized services that are key inputs for the management of a global network of factories, offices, and financial markets. The mobility of capital also includes the production of a broad array of innovations in these sectors. These types of production have their own locational patterns; they tend toward high levels of agglomeration. We will want to ask whether a focus on the *production* of these service inputs illuminates the question of place in processes of economic globalization, particularly the kind of place represented by cities.

Specialized services for firms and financial transactions, as well as the complex markets both entail, are a layer of activity that has been central to the organization of major global processes in the 1980s. To what extent is it useful to think in terms of the broader category of cities as key locations for such activities—in addition to the more narrowly defined locations represented by headquarters of transnational corporations or offshore banking centers—to further our understanding of major aspects of the organization and management of the world economy?

Much of the scholarly literature on cities has focused on internal aspects of the urban social, economic, and political systems, and it has considered cities to be part of national urban systems. International aspects typically have been considered the preserve of nation-states, not of cities. The literature on international economic activities, moreover, has traditionally focused on the activities of multinational corporations and banks and has seen the key to globalization in the *power* of multinational firms. Again, this conceptualization has the effect of leaving no room for a possible role by cities.

Including cities in the analysis adds two important dimensions to the study of economic internationalization. First, it breaks down the nation-state into a variety of components that may be significant in understanding international economic activity. Second, it displaces the focus from the power of large corporations over governments and economies to the range of activities and organizational arrangements necessary for the implementation and maintenance of a global network of factories, service operations, and markets; these are all processes only partly encompassed by the activities of transnational corporations and banks. Third, it contributes to a focus on place and on the urban social and political order associated with these activities. Processes of economic globalization are thereby reconstituted as concrete production complexes situated in specific places containing a multiplicity of activities and interests, many unconnected to global processes. Focusing on cities allows us to specify a geography of strategic places on a global scale, as well as the microgeographies and politics unfolding within these places.

A central thesis organizing this book is that the transformation during the last two decades in the composition of the world economy accompanying the shift to services and finance brings about a renewed importance of major cities as sites for certain types of activities and functions. In the current phase of the world economy, it is precisely the combination of the global dispersal of economic activities *and* global integration—under conditions of continued concentration of economic ownership and control—that has contributed to a strategic role for certain major cities that I call **global cities** (Sassen, 1991). Some have been centers for world trade and banking for centuries, but beyond these long-standing functions, today's global cities are (1) command points in the organization of the world economy; (2) key locations and marketplaces for the leading industries of the current period, which are finance and specialized services for firms; and (3) major sites of production for these industries, including the production of innovations. Several cities also fulfill equivalent functions on the smaller geographic scales of both trans- and subnational regions.

Alongside these new global and regional hierarchies of cities is a vast territory that has become increasingly peripheral, increasingly excluded from the major economic processes that fuel economic growth in the new global economy. A multiplicity of formerly important manufacturing centers and port cities have lost functions and are in decline, not only in the less developed countries but also in the most advanced economies. This is yet another meaning of economic globalization. We can think of these developments as constituting new geographies of centrality (that cut across the old divide of poor/rich countries) and of marginality that have become increasingly evident in the less developed world and in highly developed countries as well.

The most powerful of these new geographies of centrality binds the major international financial and business centers: New York, London, Tokyo, Paris, Frankfurt, Zurich, Amsterdam, Sydney, Hong Kong, among others. But this geography now also includes cities such as Sao Paulo and Mexico City. The intensity of transactions among these cities, particularly through the financial markets, flows of services, and investment has increased sharply, and so have the orders of magnitude involved. At the same time, there has been a sharpening inequality in the concentration of strategic resources and activities between each of these cities and others in the same country. For instance, Paris now concentrates a larger share of leading economic sectors and wealth in France than it did 20 years ago, whereas Marseilles, once a major economic center, has lost its share and is suffering severe decline. Some national capitals, for example, have lost central economic functions and power to the new global cities, which have taken over some of the coordination functions, markets, and production processes once concentrated in national capitals or in major regional centers. Sao Paulo has gained immense strength as a business and financial center in Brazil over Rio de Janeiro—once the capital and most important city in the country—and over the once powerful axis represented by Rio and Brasilia, the current capital. This is one of the meanings, or consequences, of the formation of a globally integrated economic system.

What is the impact of this type of economic growth on the broader social and economic order of these cities? A vast literature on the impact of a dynamic, high-growth manufacturing sector in highly developed countries shows that it raises wages, reduces economic inequality, and contributes to the formation of a middle class. There is much less literature on the impact on the service economy, especially the rapidly growing specialized services.

Specialized services, which have become a key component of all developed economies, are not usually analyzed in terms of a production or work process. Such services are usually seen as a type of output—that is, high-level technical expertise. Thus insufficient attention has been paid to the actual array of jobs, from high paying to low paying, involved in the production of these services. A focus on production displaces the emphasis from expertise to work. Services need to be produced, and the buildings that hold the workers need to be built and cleaned. The rapid growth of the financial industry and of highly specialized services generates not only high-level technical and administrative jobs but also low-wage unskilled jobs. Together with the new interurban inequalities mentioned above, we are also seeing new economic inequalities within cities, especially within global cities and their regional counterparts.

The new urban economy is in many ways highly problematic. This is perhaps particularly evident in global cities and their regional counterparts. The new growth sectors of specialized services and finance contain capabilities for profit making that are vastly superior to those of more traditional economic sectors. The latter are essential to the operation of the urban economy and the daily needs of residents, but their survival is threatened in a situation where finance and specialized services can earn superprofits. This sharp polarization in the profit-making capabilities of different sectors of the economy has always existed. But what we see happening today takes place on a higher order of magnitude, and it is engendering massive distortions in the operations of various markets, from housing to labor. We can see this effect, for example, in the unusually sharp increase in the beginning salaries of MBAs and lawyers and in the precipitous fall in the wages of low-skilled manual workers and clerical workers. We can see the same effect in the retreat of many real estate developers from the low- and medium-income housing market who are attracted to the rapidly expanding housing demand by the new highly paid professionals and the possibility for vast overpricing of this housing supply.

The rapid development of an international property market has made this disparity even worse. It means that real estate prices at the center of New York City are more connected to prices in London or Frankfurt than to the overall real estate market in the city. Powerful institutional investors from Japan, for instance, find it profitable to buy and sell property in Manhattan or central London. They force prices up because of the competition and raise them even further to sell at a profit. How can a small commercial operation in New York compete with such investors and the prices they can command?

The high profit-making capability of the new growth sectors rests partly on speculative activity. The extent of this dependence on speculation can be seen in the crisis of the 1990s that followed the unusually high profits in finance and real estate in the 1980s. The real estate and financial crisis, however, seems to have left the basic dynamic of the sector untouched. The crisis can thus be seen as an adjustment to more reasonable (that is, less speculative) profit levels. The overall dynamic of polarization in profit levels in the urban economy remains in place, as do the distortions in many markets.

The typical informed view of the global economy, cities, and the new growth sectors does not incorporate these multiple dimensions. Elsewhere I have argued that we could think of the dominant narrative or mainstream account of economic globalization as a narrative of eviction (Sassen, 1993). In the dominant account, the key concepts of globalization, information economy, and telematics all suggest that place no longer matters and that the only type of worker that matters is the highly educated professional. This account favors the capability for global transmission over the concentrations of established infrastructure that make transmission possible; favors information outputs over the workers producing those outputs, from specialists to secretaries; and favors the new transnational corporate culture over the multiplicity of cultural environments, including reterritorialized immigrant cultures within which many of the "other" jobs of the global information economy take place. In brief, the dominant narrative concerns itself with the upper circuits of capital, not the lower ones.

This narrow focus has the effect of excluding from the account the *place*-boundedness of significant components of the global information economy; it thereby also excludes a whole array of activities and types of workers from the story of globalization that are as vital to it as international finance and global telecommunications are. By failing to include these activities and workers, it ignores the variety of cultural contexts within which they exist, a diversity as present in processes of globalization as is the new international corporate culture. When we focus on place and production, we can see that globalization is a process involving not only the corporate economy and the new transnational corporate culture but also, for example, the immigrant economies and work cultures evident in our large cities.

The new empirical trends and the new theoretical developments have made cities prominent once again in most of the social sciences. Cities have reemerged not only as objects of study but also as strategic sites for the theorization of a broad array of social, economic, and political processes central to the current era: economic globalization and international migration; the emergence of specialized services and finance as the leading growth sector in advanced economies; and new types of inequality. In this context, it is worth noting that we are also seeing the beginning of a repositioning of cities in policy arenas. Two instances in particular stand out. One is the recent programmatic effort at the World Bank to produce analyses that show how central urban economic productivity is to macroeconomic performance. The other is the explicit competition among major cities to gain access to increasingly global markets for resources and activities ranging from foreign investment, headquarters, and international institutions to tourism and conventions.

The subject of the city in a world economy is extremely broad. The literature on cities is inevitably vast, but it focuses mostly on single cities. It is also a literature that is mostly domestic in orientation. International studies of cities tend to be comparative. What is lacking is a transnational perspective on the subject: that is to say, one that takes as its starting point a dynamic system or set of transactions that by its nature entails multiple locations involving more than one country. This contrasts with a comparative international approach, which focuses on two or more cities that may have no connections among one another.

Given the vastness of the subject and of the literature on cities and given what is lacking in much of that literature, this book focuses particularly on recent empirical and conceptual developments because they are an expression of major changes in urban and national economies and in modes of inquiry about cities. Such a choice is inevitably limited and certainly cannot account for the cases of many cities that may *not* have experienced any of these developments. Our focus on the urban impact of economic globalization, the new inequalities among and within cities, and the new urban economy is justified by the major characteristics of the current historical period and the need for social scientists to address these changes.

Chapter 2 examines key characteristics of the global economy that are important for an understanding of the impact of globalization on cities. Chapter 3 analyzes the new interurban inequalities, focusing on three key issues: (1) the impact of globalization, particularly the internationalization of production and the growth of tourism, on so-called **primate urban systems** in less developed countries; (2) the impact of economic globalization on so-called **balanced urban systems**; and (3) the possibility of the formation of a transnational urban system. A rapidly growing research literature now finds sharp increases in the linkages binding the cities that function as production sites and marketplaces for global capital. Chapter 4 focuses on the new urban economy, where finance and specialized services have emerged as driving engines for profit making. Chapter 5 examines these issues in greater detail through a series of case studies of key global cities and related issues. Chapter 6 focuses on possible new urban forms and social alignments inside these cities. Are the new social alignments inside cities merely a quantitative transformation or also a qualitative one? Chapter 7 considers this and other possibilities in summarizing the central propositions of this book.

2

The Urban Impact of Economic Globalization

Profound changes in the composition, geography, and institutional framework of the global economy have had major implications for cities. In the 1800s, when the world economy consisted largely of trade, the crucial sites were harbors, plantations, factories, and mines. Cities were already servicing centers at that time: cities typically developed alongside harbors, and trading companies were dependent on multiple industrial, banking, and other commercial services located in cities. Cities, however, were not the key production sites for the leading industries in the 1800s; the production of wealth was centered elsewhere. Today, international trade continues to be an important fact in the global economy, but it has been overshadowed both in value and in power by international financial flows, whether loans and equities or foreign currency transactions. In the 1980s, finance and specialized services have emerged as the major components of international transactions. The crucial sites for these transactions are financial markets, advanced corporate service firms, banks, and the headquarters of transnational corporations. These sites lie at the heart of the process for the creation of wealth, and they are located in cities.

Thus one of the factors influencing the role of cities in the new global economy is the change in the composition of international transactions, a factor often not recognized in standard analyses of the world economy. The current composition of international transactions shows this transformation very clearly. For instance, foreign direct investment grew three times faster in the 1980s than the growth of the export trade. Furthermore, by the mid-1980s investment in services had become the main component in foreign direct investment flows where before it had been in manufacturing or raw materials extraction. The monetary value of international financial flows is larger than the value of international trade and of foreign direct investment. The sharp growth of international financial flows has raised the level of complexity of transactions. This new circumstance demands a highly advanced infrastructure of specialized services and top-level concentrations of telecommunications facilities. Cities are central locations for both.

The first half of this chapter will present a somewhat detailed account of the geography, composition, and institutional framework of the global economy today. The second half will focus on two types of strategic places for international financial and service transactions: global cities and offshore banking centers. Finally, we will consider the impact of the collapse of the Pax Americana on the world economy and the subsequent shift in the geographical axis of international transactions.

The Global Economy Today

Here we emphasize new investment patterns and dominant features of the current period. The purpose is not to present an exhaustive account of all that constitutes the world economy today. It is rather to discuss what distinguishes the current period from the immediate past.

Geography

A key feature of the global economy today is the geography of the new types of international transactions. When international flows consist of raw materials, agricultural products, or mining goods, the geography of transactions is in part determined by the location of natural resources. Historically this has meant that a large number of countries in Africa, Latin America, and the Caribbean were key sites in this geography. When finance and specialized services became the dominant component of international transactions in the early 1980s, the role of cities was strengthened. At the same time, the sharp concentration in these industries means that now only a limited number of cities play a strategic role.

The fact of a new geography of international transactions becomes evident in foreign direct investment (FDI) flows—that is, investors acquiring a firm, wholly or in part, or building and setting up new firms in a foreign country (see UNCTD, 1993). FDI flows are highly differentiated in their destination and can be constituted through many different processes. During the last two decades, the growth in FDI has been embedded in the internationalization of production of goods and services. The internationalization of production in manufacturing is particularly important in establishing FDI flows into developing countries.

Compared to the 1950s, the 1980s saw a narrowing of the geography of the global economy and a far stronger East-West axis. This is evident in the sharp growth of investment and trade within what is often referred to as the *triad:* the United States, Western Europe, and Japan. FDI flows to developed countries grew at an average annual rate of 24 percent from

1986 to 1990, reaching a value of US$172 billion in 1990, out of a total worldwide FDI inflow of US$203 billion (see Table 2.1). By the mid-1980s, 75 percent of all FDI stock and 84 percent of FDI stock in services was in developed countries. There is a sharp concentration even among developed countries in these patterns: the top four recipient countries (United States, United Kingdom, France, and Germany) accounted for half of world inflows in the 1980s; the five major exporters of capital (United States, United Kingdom, Japan, France, and Germany) accounted for 70 percent of total outflows. Financial concentration is evident in a ranking of the top banks in the world (see Table 2.2 and also Chapter 5).

Although investment growth rates in developing countries were far lower than in developed countries, they were high in absolute terms—a fact that reflects the growing internationalization of economic activity (see Table 2.1). International investment in developing countries lost share in the 1980s, although it increased in absolute value and regained share in the early 1990s. Since 1985 FDI has been growing at an annual rate of 22 percent, compared to 3 percent from 1980 to 1984, and 13 percent from 1975 to 1979. Yet the share of worldwide flows going to developing countries as a whole fell from 26 percent to 17 percent between the early 1980s and the late 1980s, pointing to the strength of flows within the triad (United States, Western Europe, and Japan). Most of the flow to developing countries has gone into East, South, and Southeast Asia, where the annual rate of growth rose on the average by 37 percent a year between 1985 and 1989.

There was a time when Latin America was the single largest recipient region of FDI. Between 1985 and 1989, Latin America's share of total flows to developing countries fell from 49 percent to 38 percent, and Southeast Asia's share rose from 37 percent to 48 percent. However, the absolute increase in FDI has been so sharp that, notwithstanding a falling share, Latin America has actually experienced increases in the amount of FDI, especially toward the end of the 1980s and early 1990s (although these increases are mostly concentrated in a few countries). These figures point to the emergence of Southeast Asia as a crucial transnational space for production. The Asian region has surpassed Latin America and the Caribbean for the first time ever as the largest host region for FDI in developing countries.

Composition

In the 1950s, the major international flow was world trade, concentrated in raw materials, other primary products, and resource-based manufacturing. In the 1980s, the gap between the growth rate of exports and that

TABLE 2.1

Inflows and Outflows of Foreign Direct Investment, 1987–1992 (billions of dollars and percentage)

Country	Billions of Dollars						Share in Total (Percentage)				Growth Rate (Percentage)			
	1987	1988	1989	1990	1991	1992[a]	1981–1985	1986–1990	1991	1992	1981–1985	1986–1990	1991	1992
Developed countries														
Inflows	109	132	167	172	108	86	74	83	74	68	0.2	24	−37	−20
Outflows	132	162	203	225	177	145	98	97	97	97	3	24	−21	−18
Developing economies														
Inflows	25	30	29	31	39	40	26	17	26	32	−4	14	21	3
Outflows	2	6	10	9	5	5	2	3	3	3	33	45	−39	0
All countries														
Inflows	135	162	196	203	149	126	100	100	100	100	−0.9	22	−27	−15
Outflows	135	168	213	234	183	150	100	100	100	100	4	24	−22	−18

[a]Based on preliminary estimates.

Source: UNCTAD, Programme on Transnational Corporations (1993), p. 16.

TABLE 2.2

Top 30 Banks in the World Ranked by Assets, 1991[a]

Asset Rank	Bank	City	Country
1	Dai-Ichi Kangyo Bank Ltd.	Tokyo	Japan
2	Sumitomo Bank Ltd.	Osaka	Japan
3	Sakura Bank Ltd.	Tokyo	Japan
4	Fuji Bank Ltd.	Tokyo	Japan
5	Sanwa Bank Ltd.	Osaka	Japan
6	Mitsubishi Bank Ltd.	Tokyo	Japan
7	Norinchukin Bank	Tokyo	Japan
8	Credit Agricole Mutuel	Paris	France
9	Credit Lyonnais	Paris	France
10	Industrial Bank of Japan Ltd.	Tokyo	Japan
11	Deutsche Bank AG	Frankfurt	Germany
12	Banque Nationale de Paris	Paris	France
13	Barclay's Bank Plc	London	United Kingdom
14	Takai Bank Ltd.	Nagoya	Japan
15	Mitsubishi Trust & Banking Corp.	Tokyo	Japan
16	ABN-AMRO Bank Ltd.	Nagoya	Japan
17	Sumitomo Trust & Banking Co. Ltd.	Osaka	Japan
18	National Westminster Bank Plc	London	United Kingdom
19	Mitsui Trust & Banking Co. Ltd.	Osaka	Japan
20	Societe Generale	Paris	France
21	Long-Term Credit Bank of Japan Ltd.	Tokyo	Japan
22	Bank of Tokyo Ltd.	Tokyo	Japan
23	Kyowa Saitama Bank Ltd.	Tokyo	Japan
24	Dresdner Bank	Frankfurt	Germany
25	Daiwa Bank Ltd.	Osaka	Japan
26	Union Bank of Switzerland	Zurich	Switzerland
27	Yasuda Trust & Banking Co. Ltd.	Tokyo	Japan
28	Istituto Bancario San Paulo di Torino	Turin	Italy
29	Citibank NA	New York	United States
30	Toyo Trust & Banking Co. Ltd.	Tokyo	Japan

[a]Banks ranked by assets on December 31, 1991, or nearest fiscal year-end. Holding companies are excluded.

Source: The American Banker, 1992.

of financial flows widened sharply. Although there are severe problems with measurement, the increase in financial and service transactions, especially the former, is so sharp as to leave little doubt (see Table 2.3). For instance, worldwide outflows of FDI nearly tripled between 1984 and 1987, grew another 20 percent in 1988, and grew yet another 20 percent in 1989. By 1990, total worldwide stock of FDI stood at US$1.5 trillion and at US$2 trillion by 1992. After the 1981–1982 slump and up to 1990, global FDI grew at an average of 29 percent a year, a historic high.

Many factors have fed the growth of FDI: several developed countries became major capital exporters, most notably Japan; the number of cross-border mergers and acquisitions grew sharply; the flow of services and transnational service corporations have emerged as major components in the world economy. Services, which accounted for about 24 percent of worldwide stock in FDI in the early 1970s, had grown to 50 percent of stock and 60 percent of annual flows by the end of the 1980s. The single largest recipient of FDI in services in the 1980s—the decade of high growth of these flows—was the European Community, yet another indication of a very distinct geography in world transactions. But it should be noted that these flows have also increased in absolute terms in the case of less developed countries.

Another major transformation has been the sharp growth in the numbers and economic weight of transnational corporations (TNCs)—firms that operate in more than one country through affiliates, subsidiaries, or other arrangements. The central role played by transnational corporations can be seen in the fact that U.S. and foreign TNCs accounted for 80 percent of international trade in the United States in the late 1980s; furthermore, more than a third of U.S. international trade was actually intrafirm trade—that is, between geographically separated units within the same company (UNCTC, 1991, Chap. 3). Almost all FDI and a large share of technology transfers are undertaken by TNCs.

Institutional Framework

How does the "world economy" cohere as a system? We cannot take the world economy for granted and assume that it exists simply because international transactions do. One question raised by the developments described above is whether the global economic activities occurring today represent a mere quantitative change or actually entail a change in the international regime governing the world economy. Elsewhere I have argued that the ascendance of international finance and services produces a new regime with distinct consequences for other industries, especially manufacturing, and for regional development, insofar as regions tend to be dominated by particular industries (Sassen, 1991). One consequence of this new regime is that transnational corporations have become even more central to the organization of the world economy, and the new, or vastly expanded older, global markets are now an important element in the institutional framework.

In addition to financing huge government deficits, the financial credit markets that exploded into growth in the 1980s served the needs of TNCs to a disproportionate extent. Transnational corporations also emerged as a source for financial flows to developing countries, both through direct inflows of FDI and indirectly, insofar as FDI stimulates other forms of financial flows. In some respects, TNCs replaced banks.[1] The bank crisis of 1982 sharply cut bank loans to developing countries to the point that the aggregate net flow of financial resources to developing countries was negative during much of the 1980s. For better or for worse, the transnational corporation is now a strategic organizer of what we call the world economy.

Global financial markets have emerged as yet another crucial institution organizing the world economy. The central role of markets in international finance, a key component of the world economy today, was in part brought about by the so-called third-world bank crisis formally declared in 1982. This was a crisis for the major transnational banks in the United States, which had made massive loans to third-world countries and firms incapable of repayment. The crisis created a space into which small, highly competitive financial firms moved, launching a whole new era during the 1980s in speculation, innovation, and levels of profitability. The result was a highly unstable period, but one with almost inconceivably high levels of profits that fed a massive expansion in the volume of international financial transactions. Deregulation was another key mechanism facilitating this type of growth, centered in internationalization and in speculation. Markets provided an institutional framework that organized these massive financial flows.

The formation of transnational trading blocs is yet another development that contributes to the new institutional framework. The two major blocs now approved are the North American Free Trade Agreement (NAFTA) and the European Economic Community (EEC). (There has been relatively little discussion of the formal institutionalization of the

---

[1]FDI by transnationals may be financed through transnational banks or through the international credit markets. The mid-1980s saw a sharp increase in the share of the latter and a sharp decline in the former (see Sassen, 1991, Chap. 4).

TABLE 2.3

Sectoral Distribution of FDI Stock for the Largest Developed Home Countries and the Largest Developed and Developing Host Countries, 1970–1990 (billions of dollars and percentage)

Group of Countries and Sectors	Billions of Dollars					Average Annual Growth Rate in Percent					Share in Percentage				
	1970	1975	1980	1985	1990	1971–1975	1976–1980	1981–1985	1986–1990	1981–1990	1970	1975	1980	1985	1990
A. Outward stock															
Developed countries[a]															
Primary	29	58	88	115	160	14.0	8.7	5.5	6.8	6.2	22.7	25.3	18.5	18.5	11.2
Secondary	58	103	208	240	556	11.7	15.1	2.9	18.3	10.3	45.2	45.0	43.8	38.7	38.7
Tertiary	41	68	179	265	720	10.4	21.4	8.2	22.1	14.9	31.4	27.7	37.7	42.8	50.1
Total	129	229	475	620	1436	11.7	15.7	5.5	18.3	11.7	100.0	100.0	100.0	100.0	100.0
B. Inward stock															
Developed countries[b]															
Primary	12	17	18	39	94	4.7	5.9	16.7	19.2	18.0	16.2	12.1	6.7	9.2	9.1
Secondary	44	79	148	195	439	10.7	13.4	5.7	17.6	11.5	60.2	56.5	55.2	46.2	42.5
Tertiary	17	44	102	188	499	16.5	18.3	13.0	21.6	17.2	23.7	31.4	38.1	44.5	48.4
Total	73	140	268	422	1032	11.3	13.9	9.5	19.6	14.4	100.0	100.0	100.0	100.0	100.0

TABLE 2.3 (CONTINUED)

Group of Countries and Sectors	Billions of Dollars					Average Annual Growth Rate in Percent					Share in Percentage				
	1970	1975	1980	1985	1990	1971–1975	1976–1980	1981–1985	1986–1990	1981–1990	1970	1975	1980	1985	1990
Developing countries/ economies[c]															
Primary	—	7	17	31	46	—	19.4	12.8	8.2	10.5	—	20.6	22.7	24.0	21.9
Secondary	—	19	41	64	102	—	16.6	9.3	9.8	9.5	—	55.9	54.6	49.6	48.6
Tertiary	—	8	17	34	62	—	16.3	14.9	12.8	13.8	—	23.5	22.7	26.4	29.5
Total	—	34	75	129	210	—	17.1	11.4	10.2	10.8	—	100.0	100.0	100.0	100.0

[a] Australia, Canada, France, Federal Republic of Germany, Italy, Japan, Netherlands, United Kingdom, and United States; together these countries accounted for almost 90 percent of outward FDI stock in 1990. 1970 and 1971–1975 growth data exclude Australia and France.

[b] Australia, Canada, France, Federal Republic of Germany, Italy, Japan, Netherlands, United Kingdom, Spain, and United States; together these countries accounted for approximately 72 percent of total inward FDI stock in 1990. 1970 and 1971–1975 growth data exclude Australia, France, and Spain.

[c] Argentina, Brazil, Chile, China, Colombia, Hong Kong, Indonesia, Malaysia, Mexico, Nigeria, Philippines, Republic of Korea, Singapore, Taiwan Province of China, Thailand, and Venezuela; together these countries accounted for 68 percent of total inward FDI in developing countries.

Source: UNCTAD, Programme on Transnational Corporations (1993), p. 62.

Asian bloc in Japan's zone of influence.) The specifics of each of the two major trading blocs currently being implemented vary considerably, but both strongly feature the enhanced capability for capital to move across borders. Crucial to the design of these blocs is the free movement of financial services. Trade, although it has received far more attention, is less significant; there already is a lot of trade among the countries in each bloc, and tariffs are already low for many goods. The NAFTA and EEC blocs represent a further formalization of capital as a transnational category, one that operates on another level from that represented by TNCs and global financial markets.

These realignments have had pronounced consequences. One consequence of the extremely high level of profitability in the financial industry, for example, was the devaluing of manufacturing as a sector—although not necessarily in all sub-branches. Much of the policy around deregulation had the effect of making finance so profitable that it took investment away from manufacturing. Finance also contains the possibility for superprofits by maximizing the circulation of and speculation in money—that is, buying and selling—in a way that manufacturing does not (for example, securitization, multiple transactions over a short period of time, selling debts). Securitization, which played a crucial role, refers to the transformation of various types of financial assets and debts into marketable instruments. The 1980s saw the invention of numerous ways to securitize debts. An agent can bundle a large number of mortgages and sell the bundle many times, even though the number of houses involved stays the same. This option is basically not available in manufacturing. The good is made and sold; once it enters the realm of circulation, it enters another set of industries, or sector of the economy, and the profits from subsequent sales accrue to these sectors.

These changes in the geography and in the composition of international transactions, and the framework through which these transactions are implemented, have contributed to the formation of new strategic sites in the world economy. This is the subject of the next section.

Strategic Places

Three types of places above all others probably symbolize the new forms of economic globalization: export processing zones, offshore banking centers, and global cities. There are also many other locations where international transactions materialize. Certainly harbors continue to be strategic in a world of growing international trade and in the formation of regional blocs for trade and investment. And massive industrial districts in major manufacturing export countries, such as the United States, Japan, and Germany, are in many ways strategic sites for international activity and specifically for production for export. None of these locations, however, captures the prototypical image of today's global economy.

Much has been published about export processing zones, and they entail types of activity less likely to be located in cities than finance and services; hence we will not examine them in detail. Suffice it to say that they are zones in low-wage countries where firms from developed countries can locate factories to process and/or assemble components brought in from and reexported to the developed countries from where they came. Special legislation was passed in several developed countries to make this possible. The central rationale for these zones is access to cheap labor for the labor-intensive stages of a firm's production process. Tax breaks and lenient workplace standards in the zones are additional incentives. These zones are a key mechanism in the internationalization of production.

Here we will focus briefly on global cities and offshore banking centers.

Global Cities

Global cities are key sites for the advanced services and telecommunications facilities necessary for the implementation and management of global economic operations. They also tend to concentrate the headquarters of firms, especially firms that operate in more than one country. The growth of international investment and trade and the need to finance and service such activities have fed the growth of these functions in major cities. The erosion of the role of the government in the world economy, which was much larger when trade was the dominant form of international transaction, has displaced some of the organizing and servicing work to specialized service firms and global markets in services and finance. Here we briefly examine these developments, first by presenting the concept of the global city and then by empirically describing the concentration of major international markets and firms in various cities.

The specific forms assumed by globalization over the last decade have created particular organizational requirements. The emergence of global markets for finance and specialized services, along with the growth of investment as a major type of international transaction, has contributed to the expansion in command functions and in the demand for specialized services for firms. Much of this activity is not encompassed by the organizational form of the transnational corporation or bank, even though these types of firms account for a disproportionate share of international flows. Nor is much of this activity encompassed by the power of transnationals, a power often invoked to explain the fact of economic globalization. It involves, rather, questions of production and of place. Here some of the hypotheses developed in our recent work are of interest, especially those that examine the spatial and organizational forms of economic globalization and the actual work of running transnational economic operations (Sassen, 1991). This way of framing the inquiry has the effect of recovering the centrality of place and work in processes of economic globalization.

A central proposition in the research literature on global cities (Sassen, 1991; Friedmann & Wolff, 1982; Friedmann, 1986) posits that the *combination* of geographic dispersal of economic activities and system integration that lies at the heart of the current economic era has contributed to a strategic role for major cities. Rather than becoming obsolete because of the dispersal made possible by information technologies, cities instead concentrate command functions. To this role I have added two additional functions: (1) cities are postindustrial production sites for the leading industries of this period, finance and specialized services; and (2) cities are transnational marketplaces where firms and governments can buy financial instruments and specialized services.

The territorial dispersal of economic activity at the national and world scale implied by globalization has created new forms of concentration. This territorial dispersal and ongoing concentration in ownership can be inferred from some of the figures on the growth of transnational enterprises and their affiliates. Table 2.4 shows how vast the numbers of affiliates of transnational corporations are.

In the case of the financial industry, we see a similar dynamic of global integration: more and more cities and a simultaneous increase of concentration at the top. We can identify two distinct phases. Up to the end of the 1982 third-world debt crisis, the large transnational banks dominated the financial markets in terms of both the volume and the nature of financial transactions. After 1982, this dominance was increasingly challenged by other financial institutions and the major innovations they produced. These challenges led to a transformation in the leading components of the financial industry, a proliferation of financial institutions, and the rapid internationalization of financial markets. The marketplace and the advantages of agglomeration—and hence, cities—assumed new

TABLE 2.4

Number of Parent Transnational Corporations and Foreign Affiliates, by Area and Country, 1990/1992

	Parent Corporations Based in Country	*Foreign Affiliates Located in Country*	*Year*
All Developed Countries	**33,500**	**81,800**	
Select Countries			
Australia	1,036	695	1992
Canada	1,308	5,874	1991
France	2,056	6,870	1990
Germany (Fed. Rep.)	6,984	11,821	1990
Japan	3,529	3,150	1992
Netherlands	1,426	2,014	1992
Sweden	3,529	2,400	1991
Switzerland	3,000	4,000	1985
United Kingdom	1,500	2,900	1991
United States	3,000	14,900	1990
All Developing Countries	**2,700**	**71,300**	
Select Countries			
Brazil	566	7,110	1992
China	379	15,966	1989
Colombia	—	1,041	1987
Hong Kong	500	2,828	1991
Indonesia	—	1,064	1988
Mexico	—	8,953	1989
Philippines	—	1,952	1987
Republic of Korea	1,049	3,671	1991
Saudi Arabia	—	1,461	1989
Singapore	—	10,709	1986
Taiwan Province of China	—	5,733	1990
Former Yugoslavia	112	3,900	1991
Central and Eastern Europe	**400**	**21,800**	
Commonwealth of Independent States[a]	68	3,900	1992
World Total	**36,600**	**174,900**	

[a]Relates to the whole of the economic territory of the former USSR.

Source: Based on UNCTAD (1993), pp. 20–21.

significance in the 1980s. These developments led simultaneously to (1) the incorporation of a multiplicity of markets all over the world into a global system that fed the growth of the industry after the 1982 debt crisis, and (2) new forms of concentration, specifically the centralization of the industry in a few leading financial centers. Hence, in the case of the financial industry, to focus only on the large transnational banks would exclude precisely those sectors of the industry where much of the new growth and production of innovations has occurred. Also, it would again leave out an examination of the wide range of activities, firms, and markets that constituted the financial industry in the 1980s.

The geographic dispersal of plants, offices, and service outlets and the integration of a growing number of stock markets around the world could have been accompanied by a corresponding decentralization in control and central functions. But this has not happened.

If we organize some of the evidence on financial flows according to the places where the markets and firms are located, we can see distinct patterns of concentration. The evidence on the locational patterns of banks and securities houses points to sharp concentration. For example, the worldwide distribution of the 100 largest banks and 25 largest securities houses shows that Japan, the United States, and the United Kingdom accounted for 39 and 23 of each, respectively (see Tables 2.5 and 2.6). This pattern persists in the 1990s, notwithstanding multiple financial crises.

The stock market illustrates this pattern well. From Bangkok to Buenos Aires, governments deregulated their stock markets to allow

TABLE 2.5

United States, Japan, and United Kingdom Shares of World's Largest 100 Banks, 1991 (in US$ millions)

	N	Assets	Capital
Japan	27	6,572,416	975,192
United States	7	913,009	104,726
United Kingdom	5	791,652	56,750
Subtotal	39	8,277,077	1,136,668
All other countries	61	7,866,276	1,263,771
Total	100	16,143,353	2,400,439

Source: Based on *The Wall Street Journal*, September 24, 1992, R27.

TABLE 2.6

United States, Japan, and United Kingdom Shares of
Largest 25 Securities Firms, 1991 (in US$ millions)

	N	*Assets*	*Capital*
Japan	10	171,913	61,871
United States	11	340,558	52,430
United Kingdom	2	44,574	3,039
Subtotal	23	557,045	117,340
All other countries	2	6,578	5,221
Total	25	563,623	122,561

Source: Based on *The Wall Street Journal*, September 24, 1992, R27.

their participation in a global market system. Yet there is immense concentration in leading stock markets in terms of worldwide capitalization—that is, the value of publicly listed firms. The market value of
equities in domestic firms confirms the leading position of a few cities
(see Table 2.7). In September 1987, before the stock market crisis, this
value stood at US$2.8 trillion in the United States and at US$2.89 trillion
in Japan. Third ranked was the United Kingdom, with US$728 billion.
The extent to which these values represent extremely high levels is indicated by the fact that the next largest value was for West Germany, a major economy where domestic equities nonetheless represented 23 percent
of GNP and capitalization stood at US$255 billion, a long distance from
the top three.

What these levels of stock market capitalization represent in the top
countries is indicated by a comparison with GNP figures: in Japan, stock
market capitalization was the equivalent of 64 percent; in the United
States, the equivalent of 119 percent; and in the United Kingdom, the
equivalent of 118 percent of GNP. The concentration in the operational
side of the financial industry is made evident in the fact that most of the
stock market transactions in the leading countries are concentrated in a
few stock markets. The Tokyo exchange accounts for 90 percent of equities trading in Japan. New York accounts for about two-thirds of equities
trading in the United States; and London accounts for most trading in
the United Kingdom. There is, then, a disproportionate concentration of
worldwide capitalization in a few cities.

TABLE 2.7

Select Stock Exchanges: Market Size, 1990

	Market Value (US$ millions)		Listed Companies (N)		Member Firms (N)
	Stocks	Bonds	Domestic	Foreign	
New York	2,692,123	1,610,175	1,678	96	516
Tokyo	2,821,660	978,895	1,627	125	124
United Kingdom (mostly London)	858,165	576,291	1,946	613	410
Frankfurt	341,030	645,382	389	354	214
Paris	304,388	481,073	443	226	44
Zurich	163,416	158,487	182	240	27
Toronto	241,925	—	1,127	66	71
Amsterdam	148,553	166,308	260	238	152
Milan	148,766	588,757	220	—	113
Australia	108,628	46,433	1,085	37	90
Hong Kong	83,279	656	284	15	686
Singapore	34,268	98,698	150	22	26
Taiwan	98,854	6,551	199	—	373
Korea	110,301	71,353	699	—	25

Source: Tokyo Stock Exchange 1992 Fact Book, April 1992. Tokyo: International Affairs Department, Tokyo Stock Exchange.

Certain aspects of the territorial dispersal of economic activity may have led to some dispersal of profits and ownership. Large firms, for example, have increased their subcontracting to smaller firms worldwide, and many national firms in the newly industrializing countries have grown rapidly, thanks to investment by foreign firms and access to world markets, often through arrangements with transnational firms. Yet this form of growth is ultimately part of a chain in which a limited number of corporations continue to control the end product and reap most of the profits associated with selling on the world market. Even industrial homeworkers in remote rural areas are now part of that chain (Sassen, 1988, Chap. 4).

Under these conditions, the territorial dispersal of economic activity creates a need for expanded central control and management if this dispersal is to occur along with continued economic concentration. This in turn has contributed to the strategic role played by major cities in the world economy today.

Offshore Banking Centers

Offshore financial centers are another important spatial point in the worldwide circuits of financial flows. Such centers are above all else tax shelters, a response by private sector actors to government regulation. They began to be implemented in the 1970s, although international tax shelters have existed in various incipient forms for a long time. The 1970s marked a juncture between growing economic internationalization and continuing government control over the economy in developed countries, partly a legacy of the major postwar reconstruction efforts in Europe and Japan. Offshore banking centers are, to a large extent, paper operations. The Cayman Islands, for example, house over $250 billion in bank liabilities (International Monetary Fund data). But even though that tiny country supposedly has well over 500 banks from all around the world, only 69 banks have offices there, and only 6 are "real" banks for cashing and depositing money and other transactions. Many of the others exist only as folders in a cabinet (Roberts, forthcoming; Walter, 1989).

These offshore centers are located in many parts of the world. The majority of Asian offshore centers are located in Singapore and Hong Kong; Manila and Taipei are also significant centers. In the Middle East, Bahrain took over from Beirut in 1975 as the main offshore banking center. Other less important centers are Kuwait, Dubai, Malta, and Cyprus. In the South Pacific, we find major centers in Australia and New Zealand and smaller offshore clusters in Vanuatu, the Cook Islands, and Nauru; Tonga and Western Samoa are seeking to become such centers. In the Indian Ocean, centers cluster in the Seychelles and in Mauritius. In Europe, Switzerland tops the list, and Luxembourg is a major center; others are Cyprus, Madeira, Malta, the Isle of Man, and the Channel Islands. Several small places are struggling to compete with established centers: Gibraltar, Monaco, Liechtenstein, Andorra, and Campione. The Caribbean has Bermuda, the Cayman Islands, Bahamas, Turks and Caicos, and the British Virgin Islands.

Why do offshore banking centers exist? This question is especially pertinent given the massive deregulation of major financial markets in the 1980s and the establishment of "free international financial zones" in several major cities in highly developed countries. The best example of such free international zones for financial activity is the Euromarket, beginning in the 1960s and much expanded today, with London at the center of the Euromarket system. Other examples, as of 1981, were international banking facilities in the United States, mostly in New York City, that allowed U.S. banks to establish special adjunct facilities to accept deposits from foreign entities free of reserve requirements and interest rate limitations. Tokyo, finally, saw the development of a facility in 1986 that allowed transactions in the Asian dollar market to be carried out in that city; this meant that Tokyo got some of the capital being transacted in Hong Kong, Singapore, and Bahrain, all Asian dollar centers.

Compared to the major international centers, offshore banking centers offer certain types of additional flexibility: secrecy, openness to "hot" money and to certain "legitimate" options not quite allowed in the deregulated markets of major financial centers, and tax minimization strategies for international corporations. Thus offshore centers are used not only for Euromarket transactions but also for various accounting operations aimed at tax avoidance or minimization.

In principle, the Euromarkets of London are part of the offshore markets. They were set up to avoid the system for regulating exchange rates and balance-of-payments imbalances contained in the Bretton Woods agreement of 1945. The Bretton Woods agreement set up a legal framework for the regulation of international transactions, such as foreign currency operations, for countries or banks wanting to operate internationally. Euromarkets were initially a Eurodollar market, where banks from the United States and other countries could do dollar transactions and avoid U.S. regulations. Over the last decade, other currencies have joined.

In finance, *offshore* does not always mean overseas or foreign; basically the term means that less regulation takes place than "onshore"— the latter describing firms and markets not covered by this special legislation. The onshore and offshore markets compete with each other. Deregulation in the 1980s brought a lot of offshore capital back into onshore markets, especially in New York and London—a not insignificant factor in convincing governments in these countries to proceed with deregulation of the financial markets in the 1980s. London's much-noted "Big Bang" and the less-noted "petit bang" in Paris are instances of such a process of deregulation of financial markets.

The Euromarkets are significant in international finance. According to the Bank for International Settlements, the Eurocurrency markets grew from US$9 billion in 1964 to US$57 billion in 1970 and US$661 billion in 1981. The oil crisis was important in feeding this growth. By the late 1970s, the pressure for deregulation was strongly felt in the United States. In that decade, the Eurocurrency markets were important in international financial transactions; in the 1980s, it was Eurobonds and Eurosecurities— that is, bonds and securities traded "offshore," outside the standard regulatory framework. Securitization was crucial in the 1980s, contributing to growth by making liquid what had been illiquid forms of debt.

Offshore banking centers basically grew out of tax havens in the 1970s, and this is one of the ways in which they differ from the Euromarkets. Some offshore centers today are mere tax havens, whereas some old tax havens have become full-fledged offshore banking centers; many offshore centers specialize in certain branches of banking, insurance, and other financial transactions. There is a clustering of small offshore banking centers within the time zone of each of the three major financial centers (New York City, London, Tokyo); these marginal offshore centers do some servicing of business being transacted in the major centers and within that time zone. But not all offshore activity is related to major centers, nor is location of offshores totally determined by time zones.

In brief, offshore banking centers represent a highly specialized location for certain types of international financial transactions. They are also a buffer zone in case the governments of the leading financial centers in the world should decide to reregulate the financial markets. On the broader scale of operations, however, they represent a fraction of the financial capital markets now concentrated in global cities.

Conclusion: After the Pax Americana

The world economy has never been a planetary event; it has always had more or less clearly defined boundaries. Moreover, although most major industries were involved throughout, the cluster of industries that dominated any given period changed over time, contributing to distinct structurings of the world economy. Finally, the institutional framework through which the world economy coheres has also varied sharply, from the earlier empires through the quasi-empire of the Pax Americana—the period of U.S. political, economic, and military dominance—and its collapse in the 1970s.

It is in this collapse of the Pax Americana, when the rebuilt economies of Western Europe and Japan reentered the international markets, that we see emerging a new phase of the world economy. There is considerable agreement among specialists that in the mid-1970s new patterns in the world economy became evident. First, the geographical axis of international transactions changed from North-South to East-West. In this process, significant parts of Africa and Latin America became unhinged from their hitherto strong ties with world markets in commodities and raw materials. Second was a sharp increase in the weight of foreign direct investment in services and in the role played by international financial markets.

Third was the breakdown of the Bretton Woods agreement, which had established the institutional framework under which the world economy had operated since the end of World War II. This breakdown was clearly linked to the decline of the United States as the single dominant economic and military power in the world. Japanese and European multinationals and banks became major competitors with U.S. firms.

These realignments are the background for understanding the position of different types of cities in the current organization of the world economy. A limited number of major cities are the sites for the major financial markets and leading specialized services firms. And a large number of other major cities have lost their role as leading export centers for manufacturing, precisely because of the decentralization of production. This shift in roles among major cities in the new world economy will be the focus of the next chapter.

3

New Inequalities among Cities

The trends described in the preceding chapter point to the emergence of a new kind of urban system, one operating at the global and transnational regional levels. This is a system wherein cities are crucial nodes for the international coordination and servicing of firms, markets, and even whole economies that are increasingly transnational. These cities emerge as strategic places in the global economy. Most cities, however, including most large cities, are not part of these new transnational urban systems. Typically urban systems are coterminous with nation-states.

Correspondingly, with rare exceptions (Walters, 1985; Chase-Dunn, 1984), studies of city systems assume that the nation-state is the unit of analysis. We ask: What is the impact of economic globalization on national urban systems? Does the globalization of major industries, from auto manufacturing to finance, have distinct effects on different types of national urban systems? We will focus on the effects of the shift to services and economic globalization on balanced and primate urban systems, the two major types of urban systems that have been identified in the research literature on cities. Western European nations typically have been regarded as a good example of balanced urban systems; Latin American nations, as a good example of systems with high levels of primacy—that is, inordinate concentrations of population and major economic activities in one city, typically the national capital. The most recent research signals some sharp changes in these two regions.

In the first two sections of the chapter, we will examine the impact of economic globalization on these two types of urban systems. In the third section, we will turn to the emergence of **transnational urban systems**.

Impacts on Primate Systems: The Case of Latin America and the Caribbean

It is widely documented that many regions in the world—Latin America, the Caribbean, large parts of Asia, and to some extent Africa—have long been characterized by urban primacy (Abreu et al., 1989; Dogan &

Select Cities in Latin America and the Caribbean

Kasarda, 1988; Hardoy, 1975; Lee, 1989; Linn, 1983; Lozano & Duarte, 1991; Stren & White, 1989).
Primate cities account for a disproportionate share of population, employment, and GNP, a fact illustrated by the figures presented in Table 3.1. Thus, Greater Sao Paulo accounts for 36 percent of national domestic product and 48 percent of net industrial

product in Brazil. Santo Domingo accounts for 70 percent of commercial and banking transactions and 56 percent of industrial growth in the Dominican Republic. And Lima accounts for 43 percent of gross domestic product in Peru.

Primacy is not simply a matter of absolute size, nor is large size a marker of primacy. Several of the cities listed in Table 3.1 are not necessarily among the largest in the world. Primacy is a relative condition that holds within a national urban system. Some of the largest urban agglomerations in the world do not necessarily entail primacy: New York, for example, is among the 20 largest in the world, but it is not a primate city given the multipolar nature of the urban system in the United States. Further, primacy is not an exclusive trait of developing countries, even though its most extreme forms are to be found in the developing world: Tokyo and London are two cities that have elements of primacy. Finally, the emergence of so-called megacities may or may not be associated with primacy. The 20 largest urban agglomerations of the recent past and the foreseeable future include some cities that are not necessarily primate, such as New York, Los Angeles, Tianjin, Osaka, and Shanghai; and others that can be characterized as having low levels of primacy, such as Paris and Buenos Aires (see Figure 3.1).

Primacy and megacity status are clearly fed by urban population growth, a process that is expected to continue. The evidence worldwide points to the ongoing urbanization of the population, especially in developing countries. As in the developed countries, one component of urban growth in those countries is the suburbanization of growing sectors of the population. The figures in Table 3.2 show rates of urban growth in select developing countries. The higher the level of development, the higher the urbanization rate is likely to be. Thus, a country like Argentina had an urbanization rate of 84.6 percent in 1985, which is quite similar to that of highly developed countries. In contrast, Algeria's urbanization rate of 42.6 percent and Nigeria's 31 percent point to a rather different urbanization level from that in developed countries. Finally, the countries in Group IV in Table 3.2 actually have vast urban agglomerations, notwithstanding the very low rate of urbanization; they are, clearly, among the most populous countries in the world, and as a result the information conveyed by an indicator such as the urbanization rate differs from that of the more typical case in terms of overall population size.

On the subject of primacy, the literature on Latin America shows considerable convergence in the identification of major patterns, along with multiple interpretations of these patterns. Many studies note that we are

TABLE 3.1

Some Indicators of the Estimated Economic Importance of Urban Areas (in percentages)

Urban Area	Year	Population	Employment	Public Revenues	Public Expenditures	Output Measure
Brazil						
Greater Sao Paulo	1970	8.6	—	—	—	36.0 of NDP
						48.0 of net industrial product
China						
Shanghai	1980	1.2	—	—	—	12.5 of gross industrial product
Dominican Republic						
Santa Domingo	1981	24.0				70.0 of commercial and banking transactions
						56.0 of industrial growth
Ecuador						
Guayaquil[a]		13.0	—	—	—	30.0 of GDP
Haiti						
All urban	1976	24.2	15.6			57.6 of national income
Port-au-Prince	—	15.0	7.7	47.2	82.7[b]	38.7 of national income
Other urban	—	9.2	7.9	—	—	18.9 of national income
India						
All urban	1970–71	19.9	17.7[c]	—	—	38.9 of NDP
Kenya						
All urban	1976	11.9	—	—	—	30.3 of income
Nairobi	—	5.2	—	—	—	20.0 of income
Other urban	—	6.7	—	—	—	10.3 of income

T A B L E 3.1 (CONTINUED)

Urban Area	Year	Population	Employment	Public Revenues	Public Expenditures	Output Measure
Mexico						
All urban	1970	60.0			(29.0)[d]	79.7 of personal income
Federal District	—	14.2				33.6 of personal income
Pakistan						
Karachi	1974–75	6.1				16.1 of GDP
Peru						
Lima	1980	28.0				43.0 of GDP
Philippines						
Metro Manila	1970	12.0	—	45.0		25.0 of GDP
Thailand						
Metro Bangkok	1972	10.9	14.0[e]		30.5[f]	37.4 of GDP
Turkey						
All urban	1981	47.0	42.0			70.0 of GNP
Tunisia						
Tunis	1975	16.0	17.2	—	—	

[a]Guayas Province.
[b]Current expenditures only.
[c]Workers.
[d]Federal public investment only.
[e]1970 data.
[f]1969 data.

Source: Friedrich Kahnert, "Improving Urban Employment and Labor Productivity," May 1987, World Bank Discussion Paper No. 10.

FIGURE 3.1

Population of 20 Largest Agglomerations, 1970–2000

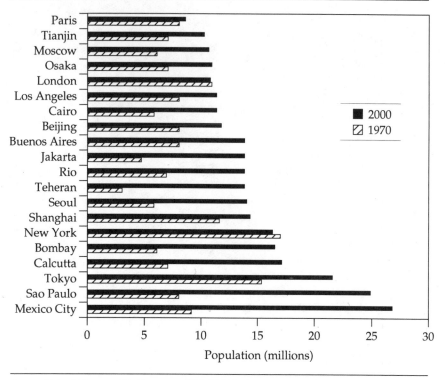

Source: United Nations, *The Prospects of World Urbanization*, 1987.

seeing sharper primacy rather than the emergence of the more balanced national urban systems we would expect with "modernization" (Edel, 1986; El-Shakhs, 1972; Roberts, 1976; Smith, 1985; Walters, 1985). The disintegration of rural economies, including the displacement of small holders because of the expansion of large-scale commercial agriculture, and the continuing inequalities in the spatial distribution of institutional resources are recognized as key factors strengthening primacy (Kowarick et al., 1991; PREALC, 1987).

Less widely known and documented is the fact that in the 1980s a deceleration in primacy occurred in several, although not all, countries in Latin America. This trend will not eliminate the growth of megacities, but it is worth discussing in some detail because it represents in part an impact of economic globalization—concrete ways in which global processes implant themselves in particular localities. The overall shift in growth strategies toward export-oriented development created growth

TABLE 3.2

Urban Growth Patterns in Select Developing Countries, 1985–2000

Group	Country	Per Capita GNP Level 1988 (US$)[a]	Size of Population (in 000's)[b] 1985 Urban	1985 Rural	2000 Urban	2000 Rural	Percentage of Urban Population[b] 1985	2000	Average Rate of Growth[b] Urban Pop. (%) 1980–1985	Urban Pop. (%) 1995–2000	Rural Pop. (%) 1980–1985	Rural Pop. (%) 1995–2000
Group I	Argentina	2,520	25,648	4,683	32,163	4,075	84.6	88.8	1.88	1.39	-0.87	-0.88
	Mexico	1,760	55,276	24,099	82,985	24,248	69.6	77.4	3.36	2.39	0.34	-0.07
	Colombia	1,180	19,357	9,357	28,557	9,441	67.4	75.2	3.11	2.29	0.28	-0.07
	Brazil	2,160	98,599	36,966	148,397	31,090	72.7	82.7	3.71	2.28	-1.27	-1.00
Group II	Algeria	2,360	9,251	12,448	16,845	16,403	42.6	50.7	3.71	3.85	2.51	1.25
	Morocco	830	9,910	12,210	17,488	13,878	44.8	55.8	4.28	3.42	1.40	0.50
	Malaysia	1,940	5,905	9,543	10,509	10,361	38.2	50.4	4.51	3.32	1.06	0.15
Group III	Senegal	650	2,343	4,101	4,301	5,366	36.4	44.5	3.34	4.26	2.11	1.52
	Ivory Coast	770	4,302	5,950	10,118	8,429	42.0	54.6	6.63	5.24	2.54	2.26
	Nigeria	290	29,556	65,643	68,893	90,256	31.0	43.3	6.07	5.33	2.22	2.02
	Sudan	480	4,502	17,316	8,902	24,708	20.6	26.5	3.99	4.88	2.88	2.19
	Kenya	370	4,002	16,351	11,937	25,645	19.7	31.8	8.06	6.72	3.17	2.78
	Zaire	170	11,248	19,464	22,875	26,474	36.6	46.4	4.41	4.73	2.29	1.80
Group IV	India	340	196,228	572,955	356,875	685,654	25.5	34.2	3.91	3.96	1.65	0.93
	Indonesia	440	42,170	124,294	75,960	132,369	25.3	36.5	4.60	3.62	1.13	0.14
	China	330	218,576	840,946	322,125	963,769	20.6	25.1	1.44	2.95	1.18	0.58

[a]The World Bank, World Development Indicators, 1990.

[b]United Nations (Department of International Economic and Social Affairs), *The Prospects of World Urbanization*, 1988.

Source: World Bank (1991), p. 20.

poles that emerged as alternatives to the primate cities for migrants (Landell-Mills et al., 1989; Portes & Lungo, 1992a, 1992b).[1] This shift was substantially promoted by the expansion of world markets for commodities and the foreign direct investment of multinational corporations.

One of the best sources of information on these developments is a large, collective, multicity study directed by Portes and Lungo (1992a, 1992b) that focused on the Caribbean region.[2] The Caribbean has a long history of urban primacy. Portes and Lungo studied the urban systems of Costa Rica, the Dominican Republic, Guatemala, Haiti, and Jamaica, countries that clearly reflect the immense variety of cultures and languages in this region. These countries represent a wide range of colonization patterns, ethnic compositions, economic development, and political stability. In the 1980s, export-oriented development, a cornerstone of the Caribbean Basin Initiative, and the intense promotion of tourism created new growth poles. The evidence suggests that these emerged as alternatives to primate cities for both the migration of workers and firms. A growth in suburbanization has also had the effect of decentralizing some of the population in the primate cities of the Caribbean, while adding to the broader metropolitan areas of these cities. The effect of these trends can be seen clearly in Jamaica, for instance, where the primacy index declined from 7.2 in 1960 to 2.2 in 1990, largely as a result of the development of the tourist industry on the northern coast of the island, the revival of bauxite production for export in the interior, and the growth of satellite cities at the edges of the broader Kingston metropolitan area.

In some Caribbean countries, however, the new growth poles have had the opposite effect. Thus, in Costa Rica, a country with a far more balanced urban system, the promotion of export manufacturing and tourism has tended to concentrate activities in the metropolitan area of the primate city of San Jose and its immediate surrounding cities, such as Cartago. Finally, in the case of Guatemala, export manufacturing and

---

[1]See also the special case of such border cities as Tijuana, which have exploded in growth because of the internationalization of production in the Mexico–U.S. border region and have become major destinations for migrants (Sanchez & Alegria, 1992). The new manufacturing free zones in China have drawn large numbers of migrants from many regions of the country (Sklair, 1985).

[2]This region is here defined as consisting of the island nations between the Florida peninsula and the north coast of South America, and the independent countries of the Central American isthmus; it excludes the large nations bordering on the Caribbean Sea.

tourism are far less developed, largely because of the extremely violent political situation (Jonas, 1992). Development of export-oriented growth is still centered in agriculture. Guatemala has one of the highest levels of urban primacy in Latin America because hardly any cities in that country have functioned as growth poles. Only recently have efforts to develop export agriculture promoted some growth in intermediate cities; thus we see that coffee and cotton centers have grown more rapidly than the capital, Guatemala City.

The growth of foreign direct investment since 1991 has further strengthened the role of the major Latin American business centers, particularly Mexico City, Sao Paulo, and Buenos Aires. As we saw in Chapter 2, privatization has been a key component of this growth (see Figure 3.2). Foreign direct investment, via both privatization and other channels, has been associated with deregulation of financial markets and key economic institutions. Thus the central role played by the stock market and other financial markets in these increasingly complex investment processes has raised the economic importance of the major cities where these institutions are concentrated. Because the bulk of the value of investment in privatized enterprises and other, often related, investments has been in Mexico, Argentina, and Brazil, the impact of vast capital inflows is particularly felt in the corporate and financial sectors in Mexico City, Buenos Aires, and Sao Paulo. We see in these cities the emergence of conditions that resemble patterns evident in major Western cities: highly dynamic financial markets and specialized service sectors; the **overvalorization** of the output, firms, and workers in these sectors; and the **devalorization** of the rest of the economic system. This is a subject we will return to in Chapter 4.

In brief, economic globalization has had a range of impacts on cities and urban systems in Latin America and the Caribbean. In some cases it has contributed to the development of new growth poles outside the major urban agglomerations: this has often been the case with the development of export manufacturing zones, agriculture for export, and tourism. In others it has actually raised the weight of primate urban agglomerations, in that the new growth poles were developed in these areas. A third case is that represented by the major business and financial centers in the region, several of which saw a sharp strengthening in their linkages with global markets and with the major international business centers in the developed world.

Production zones, centers for tourism, and major business and financial centers are three types of sites for the implantation of global processes. Beyond these sites is a vast terrain containing cities, towns, and

FIGURE 3.2

Foreign Direct Investment Inflows in Latin America, 1985–1991[a] (billions of dollars)

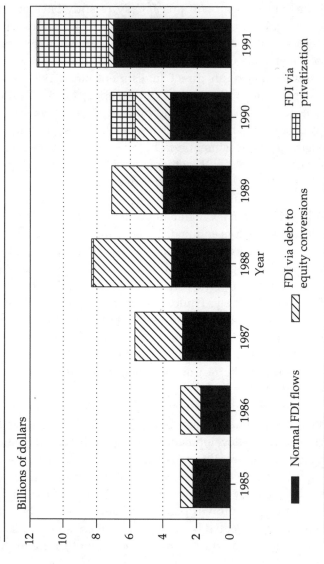

[a]Includes Argentina, Brazil, Chile, Mexico, and Venezuela, which accounted for three quarters of total FDI in the region in 1991.

Source: UNCTAD, Programme on Transnational Corporations, 1993, p. 53.

villages that is increasingly unhinged from this new international growth dynamic. Again, this dissociation is not simply a question of city size, since there are long subcontracting chains connecting workers in small villages to the world markets. It is rather a question of how these emergent transnational economic systems are articulated, how they connect specific localities in less developed countries with markets and localities in highly developed countries. The implantation of global processes seems to have contributed to increasing the separation, or disarticulation, between cities and sectors within cities that are articulated with the global economy and those that are not. This is a new type of interurban inequality. The new inequality differs from the long-standing forms of inequality present in cities and national urban systems because of the extent to which it results from the *implantation* of a global dynamic, be it the internationalization of production and finance or international tourism.

Impacts on Balanced Urban Systems: The Case of Europe

A major multiyear, multicountry study on cities in Europe, sponsored by the European Economic Community (EEC), has recently been completed. (For a summary, see European Institute of Urban Affairs, 1992, and Kunzmann & Wegener, 1991; see also Eurocities, 1989.) Perhaps one of the most interesting findings was the renewed demographic and economic importance of Europe's large cities. In the 1960s and 1970s, most if not all of these large cities had experienced declines in population and in economic activity, whereas smaller cities experienced growth in both dimensions. We saw a similar pattern in the United States, where this process took the form of suburbanization.

Many analysts both in Europe and in the United States asserted that central cities, with the exception of old historical centers with cultural importance, had lost much of their use to people and to the economy. The widespread growth of small cities in Europe in those two earlier decades was seen as a strong indication of how balanced the urban systems of Western European nations were and continue to be. And, indeed, compared to almost any other major continental region, Western European nations had and continue to have the most balanced urban systems in the world. Nonetheless, it is now clear that in the 1980s, and especially in the second half of that decade, major cities in Europe began to gain

Select Cities in Europe

population and saw significant economic growth (see Table 3.3). The exceptions were some of Europe's large cities in more peripheral areas: there were continuing losses in Marseilles, Naples, and England's old industrial cities, Manchester and Birmingham. Similarly, the rate of growth of smaller cities slowed down, often markedly.

These trends can be interpreted in several ways. On one hand, it could be argued that we are seeing mild demographic shifts that leave the characteristics of the urban system basically unaltered; that is, at the levels both of the nation and of Western Europe as a whole, we see balanced urban systems. On the other hand, it could be argued that we are

TABLE 3.3

Population Change in Select European Cities, 1970–1990

Core City[a]	1970–1975		1975–1980		1980–1985		1985–1990	
	Core	Ring	Core	Ring	Core	Ring	Core	Ring
Hamburg	−0.77	0.85	−0.91	0.36	−0.77	0.06	0.24	0.06
Frankfurt	—	—	—	—	−1.01	−0.04	1.62	0.11
Dortmund	−0.41	0.08	−0.79	−0.27	−1.15	−0.56	0.54	0.37
Berlin (West)	−1.14	0	−1.17	0	−0.49	0	2.52	0
Paris	−1.48	1.93	−0.69	0.66	−1.02	0.78	1.01	2.06
Lyons	−1.79	4.25	−1.23	1.18	0.07	−0.04	0.07	1.21
Marseilles	0.27	4.47	−0.48	2.91	−1.10	1.57	−1.10	2.84
Milan	−0.14	1.06	−1.17	1.07	−2.02	0.6	−1.03	0.35
Amsterdam	−1.84	1.51	−1.11	0.81	−1.18	0.57	0.34	0.47
Rotterdam	−1.99	1.1	−1.38	0.81	−0.28	0.56	0.22	0.28
Brussels	−1.99	0.48	−1.38	0.15	−0.95	0.02	−0.17	0.04
London	−1.89	−0.37	−1.6	−0.14	−0.38	−0.06	0.56	−0.32
Birmingham	−0.3	0.35	−1.01	−0.66	−0.33	0	−0.37	0.06
Glasgow	−3.38	−1.47	−1.84	−0.11	−1.06	−0.17	−1.41	−0.32
Dublin	−0.41	—	−0.41	—	−1.61	—	—	—
Copenhagen	−2.28	2	−1.47	0.46	−0.59	−0.12	−0.72	0.14
Thessaloniki	2.06	—	1.44	—	0.93	0.54	—	—
Athens	1.09	—	−0.16	—	−1.43	1.45	—	—
Madrid	0.45	8.28	−0.2	8.19	−0.63	3.16	0.28	0.07
Barcelona	−0.07	3.4	0.13	2.27	−0.58	0.71	0.04	−0.04
Valencia	1.44	1.47	1.11	1.73	−0.41	1.26	0.6	−0.48
Seville	1.24	−0.02	1.81	1.23	0.16	1.19	0.75	0.52
Berlin (East)	0.21	−0.05	1.14	0.14	0.9	0.06	1.85	0.17

[a]Core City refers to cities in growth or dynamic regions in Western Europe.

Source: Based on *A Report to the Commission of the European Communities, Directorate General for Regional Policy (XVI),* April 1992, p. 56.

seeing a renewed importance of major cities because the economic changes evident in all developed countries have organizational and spatial implications for such cities. The EEC study referred to earlier findings that the second of these interpretations fits the data gathered for 24 cities in Europe (see Table 3.4; see also Eurocities, 1989).

TABLE 3.4

Location of Europe's Top Banking, Industrial, and Commercial Firms, 1990

City	Banks (Number)	Commercial Firms (Number)	Industrial Firms (Number)
London	13	49	85
Paris	13	19	72
Amsterdam	3	4	5
Berlin	3	—	4
Birmingham	—	—	5
Brussels	7	4	7
Copenhagen	6	4	6
Dortmund	—	1	2
Glasgow	—	1	2
Hamburg	2	8	13
Rotterdam	—	5	1
Liverpool	—	—	—
Frankfurt	12	7	9
Milan	7	—	—
Barcelona	3	—	—
Lyons	—	1	1
Madrid	7	—	—
Marseilles	—	—	—
Athens	3	—	—
Bari	—	—	1
Dublin	2	—	—
Naples	1	1	—

Source: Based on *A Report to the Commission of the European Communities, Directorate General for Regional Policy (XVI)*, April 1992, pp. 13–15.

The organizational and spatial implications of the new economic trends assume distinct forms in various urban systems. Some cities become part of transnational networks, whereas others become unhinged from the main centers of economic growth in their regions or nations. A review of the EEC report, as well as other major studies on cities in Europe, suggests that we can identify at least three tendencies in the reconfiguration of urban systems in Western Europe. First, several sub-European regional systems have emerged (CEMAT, 1988; Kunzmann &

Wegener, 1991). Second, within the territory of the European Economic Community and several immediately adjacent nations (Austria, Denmark, Greece), a limited number of cities have strengthened their role in an emergent European urban system. Finally, a few of these cities are also part of an urban system that operates at the global level.

The urban system within European nations is also being affected by these developments. The traditional national urban networks are changing. Cities that were once dominant in their nation may lose that importance, while cities in border regions or transportation hubs may gain a new importance. Furthermore, the new European global cities may capture some of the business, demands for specialized services, and investments that previously went to national capitals or major provincial cities. Cities at the periphery will feel the widening gap with the newly defined and positioned geography of centrality.

Cities in peripheral regions and old port cities have basically lost ground in their national urban systems as a result of the new hierarchies (Castells, 1989; Hausserman & Siebel, 1987; Parkinson et al., 1989; Roncayolo, 1990; Siebel, 1984; van den Berg et al., 1982; Vidal, Viard, et al., 1990). They are increasingly disconnected from the major European urban systems. Some of these peripheralized cities with outmoded industrial bases have reemerged with new functions and as part of new networks—for example, Lille in France and Glasgow in the United Kingdom. Others have lost politico-economic functions and are unlikely to regain them in the foreseeable future. Yet others are becoming centers for tourism or places for second homes. A growing number of high-income Germans and English, for example, have bought country houses and "castles" in Ireland; other continental Europeans are following their example. Much of the beauty of the Irish countryside—whole regions untouched by industrialization—is a legacy of poverty. The requirement for becoming transnational centers for tourism and second homes is that these sites cannot pursue industrial development and need to preserve high levels of environmental quality.

Furthermore, changes in defense policies resulting from changes in the East will cause decline in cities that were once crucial production centers or control centers in national defense systems. Smaller port cities, or large ones that have not upgraded and modernized their infrastructures, will be at a great disadvantage in competing with the large, modernized port cities in Europe. Marseilles was once a great port, strategically located on the Mediterranean; today it has been left behind by Rotterdam and a few other major European ports that constitute a cluster of state-of-the-art ports. Nothing in the near future seems to secure the revitalization of old industrial centers on the basis of the industries that once were their economic core. The most difficult cases are small- and medium-size cities in somewhat isolated or peripheral areas dependent on coal and steel industries. They are likely to have degraded their environments and hence do not even have the option of becoming tourist centers.

Kunzmann and Wegener (1991) see the dominance of the large cities continuing in part because the competition among cities in Europe for both European and non-European investment will continue to favor the larger high-tech industrial and service cities (see also Deecke et al., 1993). Further, this spatial polarization will deepen because of the development of high-speed transport infrastructure and communications corridors, which will tend to connect major centers or highly specialized centers essential to the advanced economic system (Masser et al., 1990). For example, Lille's position in the center of Western Europe has strengthened its role as a transportation and communications hub, and this once dying industrial city is now the site of massive infrastructure projects.

We may be seeing a process of recentralization in certain cities that have been somewhat peripheral. Some of the smaller cities in Europe (such as Aachen, Strasbourg, Nice, Liege, Arnheim) are likely to benefit from the single European market insofar as they can expand their hinterland and function as a nexus to a broader European region. Changes in Eastern Europe are likely to strengthen the role of Western European cities that used to have extensive interregional linkages before World War II—notably Hamburg, Copenhagen, and Nuremberg—which in turn may have the effect of weakening the position of other peripheral cities in those regions. Cities bordering Eastern Europe may assume new roles or recapture old ones; Vienna and Berlin are emerging as international business platforms for the whole central European region.[3]

Finally, major Eastern European cities such as Budapest, Prague, and Warsaw may regain some of their prewar importance. Budapest is a good example: toward the late 1980s it emerged as the leading international business center for the Eastern European region, a role illustrated by the fact that Hungary was the major recipient of foreign direct investment in Eastern Europe (see Figure 3.3). Although the absolute investment levels

---

[3]The strengthening of Berlin, both through reunification and regaining the role of capital, may alter some of the power relations among Budapest, Vienna, and Berlin. Many analysts believe that Berlin will become the major international business center for Central Europe, with corresponding reductions in the roles of Budapest and Vienna. One could also posit that these three cities may create a regional transnational urban system for the whole region, in which both competition *and* a division of functions have the effect of strengthening the overall international business capability of the region.

FIGURE 3.3

Cumulative Foreign Direct Investment in Central and Eastern Europe, 1991 and 1992 (billions of dollars)

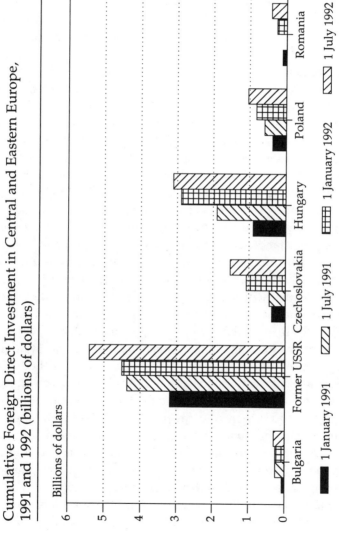

Source: UNCTAD, Programme on Transnational Corporations, 1993, p. 56.

were lower than those in the former USSR (with an immensely larger territory and economy than Hungary), in relative terms these figures represent a sharper internationalization than in the former USSR. Western European and non-European firms seeking to do business in Eastern Europe located offices in Budapest to launch operations for the region. Budapest now has a rather glamorous Western-looking international business enclave that offers the requisite comforts, hotels, restaurants, and business services in a way that most other major Eastern European cities do not yet.

Immigration is expected to grow and become a major fact in many European cities, a subject discussed in Chapter 5 (Balbo & Manconi, 1990; Brown, 1984; Canevari, 1991; Cohen, 1987; Gillette & Sayad, 1984; Tribalat et al., 1991).[4] Cities that function as gateways into Europe will receive growing immigration flows from Eastern Europe, Africa, and the Middle East. Many of these cities, particularly old port cities such as Marseilles, Palermo, and Naples, are already experiencing economic decline and will be unable to absorb the additional labor and costs (Mingione, 1991). Although these cities may function largely as entrepots, with variable shares of immigrants expected to move on to more dynamic cities, there will nonetheless be a tendency for resident immigrant populations to grow.

Having their infrastructures and services overburdened will further peripheralize these gateway cities in terms of the urban hierarchy connecting the leading cities in Europe and further contribute to polarization. On the other hand, some of Europe's global cities, such as Paris and Frankfurt, which are at the center of major transportation networks, are final destinations for many immigrants and have significant numbers in their populations and workforces (Gillette & Sayad, 1984; Body-Gendrot et al., 1992; Blaschke & Germershausen, 1989). Berlin, which according to some is an emerging global city, is also the preferred destination of many new migrations, as is Vienna. In the past, Berlin and Vienna were centers of vast regional migration systems, and they seem to be recapturing that old role. Smaller gateway cities such as Thessaloniki and Trieste seem to function more narrowly as transition posts and do not appear to be as overwhelmed as some of the other, larger gateway cities.

There are, then, a multiplicity of geographies of centers and margins in Europe at this time. A central urban hierarchy connects major cities,

---

[4]This is not an exceptional situation. All developed countries in the world now have immigrant workers. Even Japan, a country known for its anti-immigration stance, now has legal and illegal immigration, a first in its history (AMPO, 1988; Asian Women's Association, 1988; Iyotani, 1989; Morita & Sassen, 1994; Sassen, 1991, Chap. 9).

many of which in turn play central roles in the wider global system of cities: Paris, London, Frankfurt, Amsterdam, Zurich. A major network of European financial/cultural/service capitals, some with only one, others with several of these functions, articulate the European region and are somewhat less oriented to the global economy than Paris, Frankfurt, or London. And then there are several geographies of margins: the East-West divide and the North-South divide across Europe as well as new divisions. In Eastern Europe, certain cities and regions are rather attractive for purposes of both European and non-European investment, whereas others will increasingly fall behind (notably, those in Rumania, the former Yugoslavia, and Albania). We see a similar differentiation in the south of Europe: Madrid, Barcelona, and Milan are gaining in the new European hierarchy; Naples, Rome, and Marseilles are not.

Transnational Urban Systems

A rapidly growing and highly specialized research literature is focusing on different types of economic linkages that bind cities across national borders (Castells, 1989; Daniels, 1991; Leyshon, Daniels, & Thrift, 1987; Noyelle & Dutka, 1988; Sassen, 1991). Prime examples of such linkages are the multinational networks of affiliates and subsidiaries typical of major firms in manufacturing and specialized services. The internationalization and deregulation of various financial markets is yet another, very recent development that binds cities across borders. This phenomenon is illustrated by the increasing numbers of stock markets around the world that are now participating in a global equities market. There is also a growing number of less directly economic linkages, notable among which are a variety of initiatives launched by urban governments that amount to a type of foreign policy by and for cities. In this context, the long-standing tradition of designating sister cities that has recently seen sharp growth (Zelinsky, 1991) can assume a whole new meaning in the case of cities eager to operate internationally without going through their national governments.

Some of the most detailed data on transnational linkages binding cities come from studies on corporate service firms. Such firms have developed vast multinational networks containing special geographic and institutional linkages that make it possible for client firms—transnational firms and banks—to use a growing array of service offerings from the same supplier (Daniels, 1991; Leyshon et al., 1987; Noyelle & Dutka, 1988). There is good evidence that the development of transnational corporate service firms was associated with the needs of transnational firms.

The transnational advertising firm can offer global advertising to a specific segment of potential customers worldwide. Furthermore, global integration of affiliates and markets requires making use of advanced information and telecommunications technology that can come to account for a significant share of costs—not just operational costs but also, and perhaps most important, research and development costs for new products or advances on existing products.

The need for scale economies on all these fronts helps explain the recent increase in mergers and acquisitions, which has consolidated the position of a few very large firms in many of these industries and has further strengthened cross-border linkages among the key locations that concentrate the needed telecommunications facilities. These few have emerged as firms that can control a significant share of national and international markets. The rapid increase in foreign direct investment in services is strongly linked with the high level of concentration in many of these industries and a strong tendency during the 1970s toward increasing market share among the larger firms. This is particularly true for firms servicing large corporations. Subcontracting by larger firms and the multiplicity of specialized markets has meant that small independent firms can also thrive in major business centers (Parkinson et al., 1989; Sassen, 1991; Stanback & Noyelle, 1982; see also Lash & Urry, 1987).

Accounting, advertising, and legal services reflect some of these trends (Leyshon et al., 1987; Noyelle & Dutka, 1988; Thrift, 1987). In accounting, the top nine firms have increased their market share of fees for large corporate audits. The market share for small and nonaffiliated firms declined from 28 percent in 1971 to 14 percent in 1981 in the United Kingdom, from 58 percent to 1 percent in Canada, and from 64 percent to 29 percent in Australia. In the London area, four firms controlled almost two-thirds of the fees generated by the world's top nine accounting firms. Perhaps even more impressive is that the top eight firms received 40 percent of worldwide revenues; this includes very large domestic markets. Figure 3.4 shows the worldwide network of one of the top accounting firms. (See also Daniels, 1991, for a detailed account of this firm.) At the same time, however, small independent firms are also finding specialized markets and thriving in large cities such as New York and London.

In the mid-1980s, the world's five largest advertising firms controlled 38 percent of the Western European market, and about 56 percent each of the Latin American and Pacific Area market (Noyelle & Dutka, 1988, pp. 6–13). The top ten firms received 27 percent of worldwide revenues in 1987. In international legal services, there has been a growth of very large firms with multiple overseas branches and affiliates. The link between

FIGURE 3.4

Deloitte, Haskins and Sells: International Distribution of Offices and Number of Partners, 1986

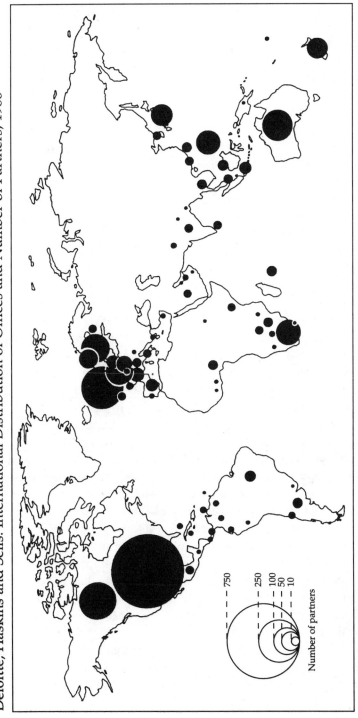

Source: Daniels (1991), p. 142.

international law firms and financial firms has contributed to a centralization of law firms in major financial centers. For instance, among the top ten foreign law firms in Hong Kong, half are from the United Kingdom and the other half are from the United States.

Whether these linkages have engendered transnational urban systems is less clear, and is partly a question of theory and conceptualization. So much of social science is profoundly rooted in the nation-state as the ultimate unit for analysis that conceptualizing processes and systems as transnational is bound to create much controversy. Even much of the literature on world or global cities does not necessarily proclaim the existence of a transnational urban system: in its narrowest form this literature posits that global cities perform central place functions at a transnational level. But that leaves open the question of the nature of the articulation among global cities. If we accept that they basically compete with each other for global business, then they do not constitute a transnational system. Studying several global cities then falls into the category of traditional comparative analysis. If we posit that, in addition to competing with each other, global cities are also the sites where transnational processes with multiple locations occur, then we can begin to explore the possibility of a systemic dynamic binding these cities.

Elsewhere (Sassen, 1991, Chap. 1 and 7) I have argued that, in addition to the central place functions performed by these cities at the global level as posited by Hall (1966), Friedmann and Wolff (1982), and Sassen-Koob (1982), these cities relate to one another in distinct systemic ways. For example, the interactions among New York, London, and Tokyo, particularly in terms of finance and investment, consist partly of a series of processes that can be thought of as the "chain of production" in finance. Thus in the mid-1980s, Tokyo was the main exporter of the raw material we call money, while New York was the leading processing center in the world. It was in New York that many of the new financial instruments were invented and that money either in its raw form or in the form of debt was transformed into instruments aimed at maximizing the returns on that money. London, on the other hand, was a major entrepot that had the network to centralize and concentrate small amounts of capital available in a large number of smaller financial markets around the world, partly as a function of its older network for the administration of the British empire.

This is just one example suggesting that these cities do not simply compete with each other for the same business. There is, it seems clear, an economic system that rests on the three distinct types of locations these cities represent. Further, it seems likely that the strengthening of transnational ties among the leading financial and business centers is accompanied by a weakening of the linkages between each of these cities and its hinterland and national urban system (Sassen, 1991). Cities such as Detroit, Liverpool, Manchester, Marseilles, the cities of the Ruhr, and now increasingly Nagoya and Osaka have been affected by the territorial decentralization of many of their key manufacturing industries at the domestic and international level. This process of decentralization has contributed to the growth of service industries that produce the specialized inputs to run spatially dispersed production processes and global markets for inputs and outputs. In a representative case, General Motors, whose main offices are in Detroit, also has a headquarters in Manhattan that does all the specialized financial work this vast multinational firm requires. Such specialized inputs—international legal and accounting services, management consulting, financial services—are heavily concentrated in business and financial centers rather than in manufacturing cities.

Conclusion: Urban Growth and Its Multiple Meanings

Major recent developments in urban systems point to several trends. In the developing world we see trends toward the continuing growth of megacities and primacy as well as the emergence of new growth poles resulting from the internationalization of production and the development of tourism. In some cases these new growth poles emerge as new destinations for migrants and thereby contribute to a deceleration in primacy; in other cases, when they are located in a primate city's area, they have the opposite effect.

In the developed world, and particularly in Western Europe, we see the renewed strength of major cities that appear to concentrate a significant and often disproportionate share of economic activity in leading sectors. In the 1970s, many of the major cities in highly developed countries were losing population and economic activity. Much was said at the time about the irreversible decline of these cities. But since then there has been a resurgence that results in good part from the intersection of two major trends: (1) the shift to services, most particularly the ascendance of finance and specialized services in all advanced economies, and (2) the increasing transnationalization of economic activity. This transnationalization can operate at the regional, continental, or global level. These two trends are interlinked and feed on each other. The spatial implications are a strong tendency toward agglomeration of the pertinent activities in major cities. This dynamic of urban growth is based largely on the locational needs or preferences of firms, whereas urban growth in less developed countries results largely from population growth, especially in-migration.

The transnationalization of economic activity has raised the intensity and volume of transaction among cities; whether this has contributed to the formation of transnational global urban systems is subject to debate. The growth of global markets for finance and specialized services, the need for transnational servicing networks in response to sharp increases in international investment, the reduced role of the government in the regulation of international economic activity and the corresponding ascendance of other institutional arenas, notably global markets and corporate headquarters—all these point to the existence of transnational economic arrangements with multiple locations in more than one country. We can see here the formation, at least an incipient one, of a transnational urban system.

The pronounced orientation to the world markets evident in such cities raises questions about the articulation with their hinterlands and nation-states. Cities typically have been and still are deeply embedded in the economies of their region, indeed often reflecting the characteristics of the latter. But cities that are strategic sites in the global economy tend, in part, to disconnect from their region. This phenomenon also conflicts with a key proposition in traditional scholarship about urban systems—namely, that these systems promote the territorial integration of regional and national economies.

Two tendencies contributing to new forms of inequality among cities are visible in the geography and characteristics of urban systems. On one hand, there is growing articulation at a transnational level among cities. This is evident both at a regional transnational level and at the global level; in some cases there are what one could think of as overlapping geographies of articulation or overlapping hierarchies that operate at more than one level; that is to say, there are cities such as Paris or London that belong to a national urban system or hierarchy, to a transnational European system, and to a global level system. On the other hand, cities and areas that are outside these hierarchies tend to become peripheralized, or become more so than they had been.

4

The New Urban Economy: The Intersection of Global Processes and Place

How are the management, financing, and servicing processes of internationalization actually constituted in cities that function as regional or global nodes in the world economy? And what is the work in terms of command functions and servicing operations at the world scale that gets done in cities?

To understand the new or sharply expanded role of a particular kind of city in the world economy since the early 1980s, we need to focus on the intersection of two major processes. The first process is the sharp growth in the globalization of economic activity discussed in Chapter 2. This economic globalization has raised the scale and the complexity of international transactions, thereby feeding the growth of top-level multinational headquarters functions and the growth of services for firms, particularly advanced corporate services. It is important to note that even though globalization raises the scale and complexity of these operations, they are also evident at smaller geographic scales and lower orders of complexity (such as firms that operate regionally). Thus, although such regionally oriented firms need not negotiate the complexities of international borders and the regulations of different countries, they are still faced with a regionally dispersed network of operations that requires centralized control and servicing.

The second process we need to consider is the growing service intensity in the organization of all industries (see Sassen, 1991, Chap. 5). This development has contributed to a massive growth in the demand for services by firms in all industries, from mining and manufacturing to finance and consumer services. Cities are key sites for the production of services for firms. Hence the increase in service intensity in the organization of all industries has had a significant growth effect on cities in the 1980s. It is important to recognize that this growth in services for firms is evident in cities at different levels of a nation's urban system. Some of these cities cater to regional or subnational markets, others cater to national markets, and yet others cater to global markets. In this context, globalization becomes a question of scale and added complexity.

The key process from the perspective of the urban economy, however, is the growing demand for services by firms in all industries and the fact that cities are preferred production sites for such services, whether at the global, national, or regional level. As a result we see in cities the formation of a new urban economic core of banking and service activities that comes to replace the older, typically manufacturing oriented office core.

In the case of cities that are major international business centers, the scale, power, and profit levels of this new core suggest that we are seeing the formation of a new urban economy. This is so in at least two regards. First, even though these cities have long been centers for business and finance, since the late 1970s there have been dramatic changes in the structure of the business and financial sectors, as well as sharp increases in the overall magnitude of these sectors and their weight in the urban economy. Second, the ascendance of the new finance and services complex, particularly in international finance, engenders what may be regarded as a new economic regime; that is, although this sector may account for only a fraction of the economy of a city, it imposes itself on that larger economy. Most notably, the possibility for superprofits in finance has the effect of devalorizing manufacturing insofar as the latter cannot generate the superprofits typical in much financial activity.

This is not to say that everything in the economy of these cities has changed. On the contrary, they still show a great deal of continuity and many similarities with cities that are not global nodes. Rather, the implantation of global processes and markets has meant that the internationalized sector of the economy has expanded sharply and has imposed a new **valorization** dynamic—that is, a new set of criteria for valuing or pricing various economic activities and outcomes. This has had devastating effects on large sectors of the urban economy. High prices and profit levels in the internationalized sector and its ancillary activities, such as top-of-the-line restaurants and hotels, have made it increasingly difficult for other sectors to compete for space and investments. Many of these other sectors have experienced considerable downgrading and/or displacement; for example, neighborhood shops tailored to local needs are replaced by upscale boutiques and restaurants catering to new high-income urban elites.

Though at a different order of magnitude, these trends were also evident during the late 1980s in a number of major cities in the developing world that have become integrated into various world markets: Sao Paulo, Buenos Aires, Bangkok, Taipei, and Mexico City are only a few examples. Also, in these cities the new urban core was fed by the deregulation of financial markets, the ascendance of finance and specialized services, and integration into the world markets. The opening of stock markets to foreign investors and the privatization of what were once public sector firms have been crucial institutional arenas for this articulation. Given the vast size of some of these cities, the impact of this new core on the broader city is not always as evident as in central London or Frankfurt, but the transformation is still very real.

In this chapter we will examine the characteristics of the new dominant sector in the urban economy of highly internationalized cities. We begin with a discussion of producer services, the core sector of the new urban economy, and the conditions shaping the growth and locational patterns of these services. We then turn to the formation of a new producer services complex in major cities, using the coordination and planning requirements of large transnational corporations as a working example of some of these issues. We also examine the locational patterns of major headquarters as a way to understand the significance of headquarters concentration in cities. We conclude with a look at the impact on the urban economy of the international financial and real estate crisis beginning at the end of the 1980s.

Producer Services

The expansion of producer services is a central feature of current growth in developed countries. In country after country we see a decline or slowdown in manufacturing alongside sharp growth in producer services. Elsewhere I have posited that the fundamental reason for this growth lies in the increased service intensity in the organization of all industries (Sassen, 1991, pp. 166–168). Whether in manufacturing or in warehousing, firms are using more legal, financial, advertising, consulting, and accounting services. These services can be seen as part of the supply capacity of an economy because they facilitate adjustments to changing economic circumstances (Marshall et al., 1986, p. 16). They are a mechanism that "organizes and adjudicates economic exchange for a fee" (Thrift, 1987) and are part of a broader intermediary space of economic activity.

Producer services cover financial, legal, and general management matters; innovation; development; design; administration; personnel; production technology; maintenance; transport; communications; wholesale distribution; advertising; cleaning services for firms; security; and storage. Central components of the producer services category are a range of industries with mixed business and consumer markets. They are insurance, banking, financial services, real estate, legal services, accounting, and professional associations.[1]

Although disproportionately concentrated in the largest cities, producer services are actually growing at faster rates at the national level in most developed economies. The crucial process feeding the growth of producer services is the increasing use of service inputs by firms in all industries. Households have also raised their consumption of services, either directly (such as the growing use of accountants to prepare tax returns), or indirectly via the reorganization of consumer industries (buying flowers or dinner from franchises or chains rather than from self-standing and privately owned "Mom-and-Pop" shops). Services directly bought by consumers tend to be located wherever population is concentrated. In that regard they are far less concentrated than producer services, especially those catering to top firms. The demand for specialized services by households, from accounting to architects, may be a key factor contributing to the growth of these services at the national level.

National figures on employment trends clearly show that the producer services are the fastest growing sector in most developed economies (see Table 4.1). Thus total employment in the United States grew from 76.8 million in 1970 to 116.9 million in 1991, but producer services grew from 6.3 to 16.35 million. In this almost threefold jump, the largest single increase was in miscellaneous business services, and the second largest was in legal services. In contrast, manufacturing only grew from 19.9 to 20.4 million. The other major growth sectors were the social services, which grew from 16.9 to 29.8 million, and personal services, from 7.7 to 13.7 million—significant levels but not nearly the rate of producer services. Distributive services also showed strong growth, from 17.2 to 24 million.

We see parallel patterns in other developed economies. Total employment in Japan grew from 52.1 million in 1970 to 61.7 million in 1990. Producer services more than doubled, from 2.5 to 5.9 million; the largest single increase was in miscellaneous business services. Manufacturing

---

[1]Mixed markets create measurement problems. These problems can be partly overcome by the fact that the consumer and business markets in these industries often involve very different sets of firms and different types of location patterns, and hence they can be distinguished on this basis. Given the existence of mixed markets and the difficulty of distinguishing between markets in the organization of the pertinent data, it is helpful to group these services under the category of "mostly" producer services—that is, services produced mostly for firms rather than for individuals. It has become customary to refer to them, for convenience, as producer services.

TABLE 4.1
National Figures on Employment Trends in Three Developed Economies, 1970–1991 (in millions)

	Japan		Germany		U.S.A.	
	1970	*1990*	*1970*	*1987*	*1970*	*1991*
I. Extractive	10,309	4,448	2,313	1,103	3,504	4,123
Agriculture	10,087	4,383	1,991	866	2,868	3,390
Mining	222	66	323	237	636	733
II. Transformative	17,772	20,795	12,481	10,835	25,310	28,824
Construction	3,943	5,906	2,033	1,908	4,634	7,087
Utilities	288	345	215	274	811	1,303
Manufacturing	13,541	14,544	10,234	8,654	19,864	20,434
Food	1,086	1,391	964	778	1,456	1,784
Textiles	1,427	714	635	307	968	688
Metal	2,103	1,985	1,243	1,168	2,391	1,992
Machinery	2,596	3,620	2,517	1,311	3,921	4,349
Chemical	666	679	634	736	1,189	1,525
Misc. mfg.	5,664	6,155	4,240	4,353	9,940	10,096
III. Distributive Services	11,689	14,987	4,748	4,765	17,190	24,079
Transportation	2,636	3,097	1,443	1,574	3,013	4,170
Communication	577	598	—	—	1,132	1,598
Wholesale	3,159	4,377	1,125	873	3,100	4,640
Retail	5,316	6,916	2,179	2,318	9,946	13,671

(continued)

TABLE 4.1 (CONTINUED)
National Figures on Employment Trends in Three Developed Economies, 1970–1991 (in millions)

	Japan		Germany		U.S.A.	
	1970	1990	1970	1987	1970	1991
IV. Producer Services	2,522	5,945	1,187	1,977	6,298	16,350
Banking	729	1,181	438	658	1,658	3,286
Insurance	376	783	244	257	1,406	2,419
Real estate	274	707	92	109	789	2,081
Engineering	268	509	163	198	333	833
Accounting	93	188	—	—	303	660
Misc. bus. serv.	741	2,493	250	754	1,401	5,797
Legal services	42	85	—	—	409	1,274
V. Social Services	5,359	8,855	4,155	6,550	16,888	29,839
Medical, health serv.	211	943	815	1,465	1,846	5,259
Hospital	923	1,328	—	—	2,836	4,839
Education	1,537	2,757	802	1,314	6,546	9,366
Welfare, relig. serv.	381	847	245	410	908	3,154
Nonprofit org.	524	656	112	56	330	468
Postal service	—	—	—	—	732	852
Government	1,759	2,092	2,053	2,545	3,484	5,639
Misc. social services	23	232	128	760	206	262

TABLE 4.1 (CONTINUED)

	Japan		Germany		U.S.A.	
	1970	1990	1970	1987	1970	1991
VI. Personal Services	4,441	6,296	1,610	1,687	7,696	13,659
Domestic serv.	153	80	116	56	1,272	1,000
Hotel	463	677	730	731	731	1,813
Eating, drinking places	1,585	2,538	—	—	2,479	5,744
Repair services	480	614	271	297	1,056	1,670
Laundry	239	349	120	62	587	470
Barber, beauty shops	565	650	234	258	728	876
Entertainment	425	822	119	248	632	1,570
Misc. personal serv.	532	567	19	35	211	516
All Other Services	19	366	—	—	—	—
Total	52,110	61,734	26,494	26,908	76,805	116,877

Source: Based on "The Space of Flows" (unpublished manuscript) by M. Castells, Department of City and Regional Planning, University of California at Berkeley.

grew from 13.5 to 14.5 million. Social services grew from 5.4 to 8.9 million, and personal services from 4.4 to 6.3 million. As in the United States, distributive services showed considerable growth, going from 11.7 to 15 million.

In France, total employment went from 20 million in 1968 to 21.8 million in 1989. Producer services doubled from 1 to 2.2 million, with the largest single increase also in miscellaneous business services. Personal services almost doubled, from 1.6 to 3 million in 1989, and social services grew from 3 to 4.3 million. Distributive services also showed strong growth, going from 3.7 to 4.5 million. Manufacturing fell from 5.4 to 4.6 million.

In the United Kingdom, total employment fell from 23.4 million in 1970 to 21.3 million in 1992. Manufacturing lost almost half of its jobs, going from 9 to 4.5 million. Distributive services remained unchanged. But, as in other developed economies, producer services more than doubled, from 1.2 million in 1970 to 2.6 million in 1992. Social services grew from 4.2 to 6.1 million and personal services from 1.9 to 2 million.

Finally, in Canada, total employment grew from 8.4 million in 1971 to 13.9 million in 1992. But producer services tripled from 0.5 to 1.6 million; miscellaneous business services accounted for two-thirds of this growth. All other service sectors also grew strongly. Distributive services almost doubled, social services grew from 1.8 to 3.1 million, and personal services grew from 0.6 to 1.9 million. Manufacturing grew from 1.6 to 2 million.

Over the last decade, producer services have become the most dynamic, fastest growing sector in many cities. Particularly notable here is the case of the United Kingdom, where overall employment actually fell and manufacturing suffered severe losses. Yet there were sharp increases in producer services in Central London between 1984 and 1987; their share rose from 31 percent to 37 percent of all employment, reaching 40 percent by 1989 (Frost & Spence, 1992). Central London saw both relative and absolute declines in all other major employment sectors. Similar developments can be seen in New York City; in 1987, at the height of the 1980s boom, producer services accounted for 37.7 percent of private sector jobs, up from 29.8 percent in 1977. There were high growth rates in many of the producer services during the period when economic restructuring was consolidated in New York City: from 1977 to 1985, employment in legal services grew by 62 percent, in business services by 42 percent, and in banking by 23 percent; in contrast, employment fell by 22 percent in manufacturing and by 20 percent in transport.

Accompanying these sharp growth rates in producer services was an increase in the level of employment specialization in business and financial services in major cities throughout the 1980s. For example, over 90 percent of jobs in Finance, Insurance, and Real Estate (FIRE) in New York City were located in Manhattan, as were 85 percent of business service jobs. If we consider only those components of producer services that may be described as information industries (even though so-called information industries can include a large share of jobs that have nothing to do with the handling of information), we can see that New York City has a significantly higher concentration than any other major American city. Information industries accounted for 31 percent of jobs in New York City in the mid-1980s, 17.8 percent in Los Angeles (county), and 20.3 percent in Chicago; all three cities show a higher incidence than the U.S. average, which stood at 15.1 percent (see also Fainstein, 1993).

Today there is a general trend toward high concentration of finance and certain producer services in the downtowns of major international financial centers around the world. From Toronto and Sydney to Frankfurt and Zurich, we are seeing growing specialization in financial districts everywhere. It is worth noting that this trend is also evident in the multipolar urban system of the United States: against all odds, New York City has kept its place at the top in terms of concentration in banking and finance (see Tables 4.2 and 4.3). Furthermore, finance and business services in the New York metro area are more concentrated in Manhattan today than they were in 1956 (Harris, 1991).[2]

These cities have emerged as important producers of services for export, with a tendency toward specialization. New York and London are leading producers and exporters in accounting, advertising, management consulting, international legal services, and other business services. They are the most important international markets for these services, with New York the world's largest source of service exports. Tokyo is emerging as an important center for the international trade in services, going beyond its initial restricted role of exporting only the services required by its large international trading houses. Japanese firms are more likely to gain a significant share of the world market in certain producer services than others (Rimmer, 1988). Construction and engineering services are examples of the first; advertising and international legal services, of the second. As recently as 1978, the United States accounted for

---

[2]Jobs are far more concentrated in the central business district in New York City, compared with other major cities in the United States: about 27 percent of all jobs in the consolidated statistical area were in Manhattan, compared with 9 percent nationally (Drennan, 1989). This still leaves the 90 percent concentration ratio of finance far above the norm.

TABLE 4.2

Assets of 50 Largest Diversified Financial Companies (in US$ millions)

City	Assets	Percentage of U.S. Top 100
Total, Top 100 U.S. Firms	1,630,258.1	—
New York	835,461.8	51.24
Chicago	23,052.6	4.23
Metro Chicago Area	45,900.9	
	(Total = 68,953.5)	
San Francisco	38,203.0	2.34
Los Angeles	1,913.8	.18
Total of Above Areas	944,532.1	57.9

Rank	City	Assets (in US$ millions)
1	New York	835,461.8
2	Washington, DC	231,977.0
3	Hartford	143,530.2
4	Philadelphia[a]	69,827.0
5	Chicago (including Metro Area)	68,953.5
6	McLean, VA[a]	59,502.0
7	Houston[a]	39,742.0
8	San Francisco	38,203.0
24	Los Angeles[a]	1,913.8

[a]Denotes cities with only one company in Top 50.

Source: "The Service 500," *Fortune*, May 31, 1993, pp. 199–230.

60 of the top 200 international construction contractors, and Japan for 10 (Rimmer, 1988); by 1985, each accounted for 34 of such firms (see Sassen, 1991, pp. 174–175).

There are also tendencies toward specialization among different cities within a country. In the United States, New York leads in banking, securities, manufacturing administration, accounting, and advertising. Wash-

TABLE 4.3

Assets of 100 Largest Commercial Banking Companies, by Region (in US$ millions)

City	Assets	Percentage of U.S. Top 100
Total, Top 100 U.S. Firms	2,500,314.8	—
New York	715,064.9	28.60
San Francisco	263,507.7	10.54
Chicago	109,760.9	4.39
Los Angeles	58,163.1	2.33
Total of Above Cities	1,146,496.6	45.9

Rank	City	Assets (in US$ millions)
1	New York	715,064.9
2	San Francisco	263,507.7
3	Charlotte, NC	169,386.0
4	Chicago	109,760.9
5	Pittsburgh	93,741.9
6	Columbus, OH	75,312.3
7	Minneapolis	68,084.1
8	Detroit	67,524.0
9	Boston	58,742.4
10	Los Angeles	58,163.1

Source: "The Service 500," *Fortune,* May 31, 1993, pp. 199–230.

ington, D.C., leads in legal services, computing and data processing, management and public relations, research and development, and membership organizations. New York is more narrowly specialized as a financial, business, and cultural center. Some of the legal activity concentrated in Washington, D.C., is actually serving New York City businesses that have to go through legal and regulatory procedures, lobbying, and so on. Such services are bound to be found in the national capital, and many are oriented to the national economy and to noneconomic purposes. Furthermore, much of the research activity in Washington is aimed not at the world economy but at national medical and health research agendas. Thus it is obviously important to distinguish whether a producer services complex is oriented to world markets and integration into the global economy or whether it responds largely to domestic demand.[3]

It is important to recognize that manufacturing remains a crucial sector in all of these economies, even when it may have ceased to be a dominant sector in major cities. Indeed, several scholars have argued that the producer services sector could not exist without manufacturing (Cohen & Zysman, 1987; Markusen & Gwiasda, 1993). In this context it has been argued, for example, that the weakening of the manufacturing sector in the broader New York region is a threat to the city's status as a leading financial and producer services center (Markusen & Gwiasda, 1993). A key proposition for this argument is that producer services are dependent on a strong manufacturing sector to grow. There is considerable debate around this issue (Drennan, 1992; Noyelle & Dutka, 1988; Sassen, 1991). Drennan (1992), a leading analyst of the producer services sector in New York City, argues that a strong finance and producer services sector is possible in New York notwithstanding decline in its industrial base; and that these sectors are so strongly integrated into the world markets that articulation with their hinterland—that is, integration with their regions—becomes secondary.

In a variant on both positions (Sassen, 1991), I argue that manufacturing indeed is one factor feeding the growth of the producer services sector, but that it does so whether located in the area in question or overseas. Even though manufacturing—and mining and agriculture, for that matter—feeds growth in the demand for producer services, its actual location is of secondary importance for global level service firms: thus, whether manufacturing plants are located offshore or within a country may be quite irrelevant as long as they are part of a multi-

---

[3]The data on producer services is creating a certain amount of confusion in the United States. For example, faster growth at the national level and in medium-size cities is often interpreted as indicating a loss of share and declining position of leading centers such as New York or Chicago. Thus one way of reading these data is as decentralization of producer services: that is, New York and Chicago are losing a share of all producer services in the United States—a zero-sum situation where growth in a new location is construed ipso facto as a loss in an older location. Another way is to read it as growth everywhere. In my reading, the evidence points to the second type of explanation: the growing service intensity in the organization of the economy nationwide is the main factor explaining growth in medium-size cities, rather than the loss of producer services firms in major cities.

national corporation likely to buy the services from top-level firms. Second, the territorial dispersal of plants, especially if international, actually raises the demand for producer services. This is yet another meaning, or consequence, of globalization: the growth of producer service firms headquartered in New York or London or Paris can be fed by manufacturing located anywhere in the world as long as it is part of a multinational corporate network. Third, a good part of the producer services sector is fed by financial and business transactions that either have nothing to do with manufacturing, as in many of the global financial markets, or for which manufacturing is incidental, as in much merger and acquisition activity (which is centered on buying and selling firms rather than the buying of manufacturing firms as such).

Some of the employment figures on New York and London, two cities that experienced heavy losses in manufacturing and sharp gains in producer services, illustrate this point. New York lost 34 percent of its manufacturing jobs from 1969 to 1989 in a national economy that overall lost only 2 percent of such jobs and that actually saw manufacturing growth in many areas. The British economy lost 32 percent of its manufacturing jobs from 1971 to 1989, and the London region lost 47 percent of such jobs (Fainstein et al., 1992; Buck, Drennan, & Newton, 1992). Yet both cities had sharp growth in producer services and raised their shares of such jobs in total city employment. Furthermore, it is also worth considering the different conditions in each city's larger region: London's region had a 2 percent decline compared to a 22 percent job growth rate in the larger New York region. This divergence points to the fact that the finance and producer services complex in each city rests on a growth dynamic that is somewhat independent of the broader regional economy—a sharp change from the past, when a city was presumed to be deeply articulated with its hinterland.

The Formation of a New Production Complex

According to standard conceptions about information industries, the rapid growth and disproportionate concentration of producer services in central cities should not have happened. Because they are thoroughly embedded in the most advanced information technologies, producer services could be expected to have locational options that bypass the high costs and congestion typical of major cities. But cities offer agglomeration economies and highly innovative environments. Some of these services are produced in-house by firms, but a large share are bought from specialized service firms. The growing complexity, diversity, and specialization of the services required makes it more efficient to buy them from specialized firms rather than hiring in-house professionals. The growing demand for these services has made possible the economic viability of a free-standing specialized service sector.

A production process takes place in these services that benefits from proximity to other specialized services. This is especially the case in the leading and most innovative sectors of these industries. Complexity and innovation often require multiple highly specialized inputs from several industries. The production of a financial instrument, for example, requires inputs from accounting, advertising, legal services, economic consulting, public relations, design, and printing. The particular characteristics of production explain the centralization of management and servicing functions that has fueled the economic boom of the early and mid-1980s in major cities. The commonly heard explanation that high-level professionals require face-to-face interactions needs to be refined in several ways. Producer services, unlike other types of services, are not necessarily dependent on spatial proximity to the consumers—that is, firms served. Rather, economies occur in such specialized firms when they locate close to others that produce key inputs or whose proximity makes possible joint production of certain service offerings. The accounting firm can service its clients at a distance, but the nature of its service depends on proximity to specialists, lawyers, and programmers. Moreover, concentration arises out of the needs and expectations of the people likely to be employed in these new high-skill jobs who tend to be attracted to the amenities and life-styles that large urban centers can offer. Frequently, what is thought of as face-to-face communication is actually a production process that requires multiple simultaneous inputs and feedbacks. At the current stage of technical development, having immediate and simultaneous access to the pertinent experts is still the most effective way to operate, especially when dealing with a highly complex product.

Furthermore, time replaces weight in these sectors as a force for agglomeration. In the past, the pressure of the weight of inputs from iron ore to unprocessed agricultural products was a major constraint pushing toward agglomeration in sites where the heaviest inputs were located. Today, the acceleration of economic transactions and the premium that is put on time have created new forces for agglomeration; that is, if there were no need to hurry, the client could conceivably make use of a widely dispersed array of cooperating specialized firms. And this is often the case in routine operations. Where time is of the essence, however, as it is today in many of the leading sectors of these industries, the benefits of agglomeration are still extremely high—to the point where it is not simply a cost advantage but an indispensable arrangement. Central here has been the general acceleration of all transactions, especially in finance, where minutes and seconds count: in the stock markets, the foreign currency markets, the futures markets, and so on.

It is just this combination of constraints that has promoted the formation of a producer services complex in all major cities. This producer services complex is intimately connected to the world of corporate headquarters; they are often thought of as forming a joint headquarters–corporate services complex. But in the analysis adopted in this book, we need to distinguish the two. Although it is true that headquarters still tend to be disproportionately concentrated in cities, many have moved out over the last two decades. Headquarters can indeed locate outside cities, but they need a producer services complex somewhere to buy or contract for the needed specialized services and financing. Headquarters of firms with very high overseas activity or in highly innovative and complex lines of business tend to locate in major cities. In brief, firms in more routinized lines of activity, with predominantly regional or national markets, appear to be increasingly free to move or install their headquarters outside cities. Firms in highly competitive and innovative lines of activity and/or with a strong world market orientation appear to benefit from being located at the center of major international business centers, no matter how high the costs.

Both types of firms, however, need a corporate services sector complex to be located somewhere. Where this complex is located is probably becoming increasingly unimportant from the perspective of many, though not all, headquarters. However, from the perspective of producer services firms, such a specialized complex is most likely to be in a city, rather than, for example, in a suburban office park. The latter will be the site for producer services firms but not for a services complex. And only such a complex is capable of handling the most advanced and complicated corporate demands.

These issues are examined in the next two sections. The first discusses how the spatial dispersal of economic activities engenders an increased demand for specialized services; the transnational corporation is one of the major agents in this process. The second section examines whether and, if so, under what conditions corporate headquarters need cities.

The Servicing of Transnational Corporations

The sharp rise in the use of producer services has also been fed by the territorial dispersal of multi-establishment firms, whether at the regional, national, or global level. Firms operating many plants, offices, and service outlets must coordinate planning, internal administration and distribution, marketing, and other central headquarters activities. As large corporations move into the production and sale of final consumer services, a wide range of activities previously performed by free-standing consumer service firms are shifted to the central headquarters of the new corporate owners. Regional, national, or global chains of motels, food outlets, and flower shops require vast centralized administrative and servicing structures. A parallel pattern of expansion of central high-level planning and control operations takes place in governments, brought about partly by the technical developments that make this expansion possible and partly by the growing complexity of regulatory and administrative tasks.

Formally, the development of the modern corporation and its massive participation in world markets and foreign countries has made planning, internal administration, product development, and research increasingly important and complex. Diversification of product lines, mergers, and transnationalization of economic activities all require highly specialized skills. A firm with a multiplicity of geographically dispersed manufacturing plants contributes to the development of new types of planning in production and distribution surrounding the firm. The development of multisite manufacturing, service, and banking has created an expanded demand for a wide range of specialized service activities to manage and control global networks of factories, service outlets, and branch offices. Although to some extent these activities can be carried out in-house, a large share is not. High levels of specialization, the possibility of externalizing the production of some of these services, and the growing demand by large and small firms and by governments are all conditions that have both resulted from and made possible the development of a market for free-standing service firms that produce components for what might be called global control capability.

This in turn means that small firms can buy components of that capability, such as management consulting or international legal advice, and so can firms and governments from anywhere in the world. This accessibility contributes to the formation of marketplaces for such services in major cities. In brief, although the large corporation is undoubtedly a key agent inducing the development of this capability and is its prime beneficiary, it is not the sole user.

A brief examination of the territorial dispersal entailed by transnational operations of large enterprises can serve to illustrate some of the points raised here. Table 4.4, for example, lists the numbers of workers employed abroad by the 25 largest nonfinancial transnational corporations worldwide. Clearly these represent rather large numbers; about a half each of Exxon's and IBM's and about a third each of Ford Motors' and GM's total workforce is employed outside the United States. We know furthermore that the 36,600 transnationals operating in 1991 have more than 170,000 affiliates (Table 2.4). More specifically, Table 4.5 shows that the leading economies in the world have a disproportionate share of affiliates. Thus in 1990, Germany had more than 19,000 affiliates in foreign countries, up from 14,000 in 1984; the United States had almost 19,000. Finally, we know that the top transnationals have very high shares of foreign operations: Table 4.6 shows that the top ten largest transnational corporations in the world had 61 percent of their sales abroad. The average for the 100 largest corporations was almost 50 percent.

What these figures show is a vast operation dispersed over a multiplicity of locations, a situation that generates a large demand for producer services, from international accounting to advertising. Operations as extensive as these feed the expansion of central management, coordination, control, and servicing functions. Some of these functions are performed in the headquarters; others are bought or contracted for, thereby feeding the growth of the producer services complex.

Corporate Headquarters and Cities

It is very common in the general literature and in some more scholarly accounts to use headquarters concentration as an indication of a city's status as an international business center. The loss of headquarters is then interpreted as a decline in a city's status. In fact, using headquarters concentration as an index is increasingly a problematic measure, given the way in which corporations are classified and the locational options telecommunications offers corporations.

A number of variables determine which headquarters concentrate in major international financial and business centers. First, how we measure or simply count headquarters makes a difference. Frequently, the key measure is the size of the firm in terms of employment and overall revenue. Using this measure, some of the largest firms in the world are still manufacturing firms, and many of these have their main headquarters in proximity to their major factory complex, which is unlikely to be in a large city because of space constraints. Such firms *are* likely, however, to have secondary headquarters for highly specialized functions in

TABLE 4.4

The 25 Largest Nonfinancial Transnational Corporations, Ranked by Foreign Assets, 1990 (US$ billions and number of employees)

Rank	Corporation	Country	Industry[a]	Foreign Assets	Total Assets	Foreign Sales	Total Sales	Foreign Employment	Total Employment
1	Royal Dutch Shell	United Kingdom/Netherlands	Petroleum refining	69.2[b]	106.4	47.1[b]	106.5	99,000	137,000
2	Ford	United States	Motor vehicles and parts	55.2	173.7	47.3	97.7	188,904	370,383
3	GM	United States	Motor vehicles and parts	52.6	180.2	37.3	122.0	251,130	767,200
4	Exxon	United States	Petroleum refining	51.6	87.7	90.5	115.8	65,000	104,000
5	IBM	United States	Computers	45.7	87.6	41.9	69.0	167,868	373,816
6	British Petroleum	United Kingdom	Petroleum refining	31.6	59.3	43.3	59.3	87,200	118,050
7	Asea Brown Boveri	Switzerland	Industrial and farm equipment	26.9	30.2	25.6[d]	26.7	200,177	215,154
8	Nestle	Switzerland	Food	—[c]	28.0	35.8	36.5	192,070	199,021
9	Philips Electronics	Netherlands	Electronics	23.3	30.6	28.8[d]	30.8	217,149	272,800
10	Mobil	United States	Petroleum refining	22.3	41.7	44.3	57.8	27,593	67,300
11	Unilever	United Kingdom/Netherlands	Food	—[c]	24.7	16.7[b]	39.6	261,000	304,000
12	Matsushita Electric	Japan	Electronics	—[c]	62.0	21.0	46.8	67,000	210,848
13	Fiat	Italy	Motor vehicles and parts	19.5	66.3	20.7[d]	47.5	66,712	303,238
14	Siemens	Germany	Electronics	—[c]	43.1	14.7[d]	39.2	143,000	373,000
15	Sony	Japan	Electronics	—[c]	32.6	12.7	20.9	62,100	112,900
16	Volkswagen	Germany	Motor vehicles and parts	—[c]	42.0	25.5[d]	42.1	95,934	268,744

TABLE 4.4 (CONTINUED)

Rank	Corporation	Country	Industry[a]	Foreign Assets	Total Assets	Foreign Sales	Total Sales	Foreign Employment	Total Employment
17	Elf Aquitaine	France	Petroleum refining	17.0	42.6	11.4[d]	32.4	33,957	90,000
18	Mitsubishi	Japan	Trading	16.7	73.8	45.5	129.3	—	32,417
19	GE	United States	Electronics	16.5	153.9	8.3	57.7	62,580	298,000
20	Du Pont	United States	Chemicals	16.0	38.9	17.5	37.8	36,400	124,900
21	Alcatel Alsthom	France	Electronics	15.3	38.2	13.0	26.6	112,966	205,500
22	Mitsui	Japan	Trading	15.0	60.8	48.1	136.2	—	9,094
23	News Corporation	Australia	Publishing and printing	14.6	20.7	4.6	5.7	—	38,432
24	Bayer	Germany	Chemicals	14.2	25.4	20.3	25.9	80,000	171,000
25	B.A.T. Industries	United Kingdom	Tobacco	—[c]	48.1	16.5[d]	22.9	—	217,373

[a]Industry classification of companies follows that in the Fortune Global 500 list in *Fortune*, 29 July 1991, and the Fortune Global Service 500 list in *Fortune*, 26 August 1991. In the Fortune classification, companies are included in the industry or service that represents the greatest volume of their sales; industry groups are based on categories established by the United States Office of Management and Budget. Several companies, however, are highly diversified.

[b]Excludes other European countries.

[c]Data for foreign assets not available; ranking is according to foreign assets estimated by the Transnational Corporations and Management Division on the basis of the ration of foreign to total employment, foreign to total fixed assets, or other similar ratios.

[d]Includes export sales which are not separately reported.

Source: Based on UNCTAD, Programme on Transnational Corporations, based on company annual financial statements, Worldscope company accounts database, unpublished sources from companies, The Industrial Institute for Economic and Social Research (Stockholm, Sweden), and Stopford, 1992. The Worldscope database uses standardized data definitions to adjust for differences in accounting terminology. Data for United States companies with fiscal year-end up to 10 February 1991, as well as for non-United States companies with fiscal year-end until 15 January 1991, are classified as 1990 data.

TABLE 4.5

Distribution of Outward Affiliates of Major Investing Countries, by Sector (number and percentage)

Country	Year		All	Primary	Manufacturing	Services
					Sectors	
Germany, Federal	1984	Number	14,657	558	4,936	9,163
Republic of[a]		Percentage	100	4	34	63
	1990	Number	19,352	422	5,729	13,201
		Percentage	100	2	30	68
Japan[b]	1980	Number	3,567	194	1,587	1,786
		Percentage	100	5	44	50
	1990	Number	7,986	194	3,408	4,384
		Percentage	100	2	43	55
United States[c]	1982	Number	18,339	995	7,005	10,339
		Percentage	100	5	38	56
	1989	Number	18,899	785	7,552	10,562
		Percentage	100	4	40	56

[a]Includes only affiliates whose balance sheet total exceeds DM 500,000.

[b]Includes only nonbank affiliates that responded to a questionnaire on FDI and that continued their foreign operations.

[c]Includes only affiliates whose assets, sales, or income exceeded $3 million.

Sources: UNCTAD, Programme on Transnational Corporations, based on Deutsche Bundesbank, 1992; Japan, Ministry of International Trade and Industry; United States Department of Commerce, 1985 and 1992.

major cities. Furthermore, many manufacturing firms are oriented to the national market and do not need to be located in a city's national business center. Thus, the much-publicized departure of major headquarters from New York City in the 1960s and 1970s involved these types of firms. If we look at the Fortune 500 list of the largest U.S. firms, we will see that many have left New York City and other large cities. If, however, instead of size we measure share of total firm revenue coming from international sales, a large number of firms that are not on the Fortune 500 list come into play. In the case of New York, for example, the results change dramatically: in 1990, 40 percent of U.S. firms with half their revenue from international sales have their headquarters in New York City.

Second, the nature of the urban system in a country is a factor in the geographic distribution of headquarters. Sharp urban primacy will tend

TABLE 4.6

Transnationalization and Concentration Ratios for the 100 Largest Transnational Corporations, by Foreign Assets and Foreign Sales, 1990 (percentage and billions of dollars)

Item	Share in Top 100 (Percentage)		Share in Top 100 (Percentage)		Share of Foreign in Total Assets (Percentage)	Share of Foreign in Total Sales (Percentage)
	Total Assets	Foreign Assets[a]	Total Sales	Foreign Sales		
Top 10	25.8	33.5	23.2	29.4	49.1	61.2
Top 25	50.0	54.4	46.0	49.2	41.1	51.7
Top 50	70.9	76.3	68.7	70.9	41.0	49.9
Top 100 Percentage	100.0	100.0	100.0	100.0	37.8	48.4
Value	3,198.6	1,208.5	3,107.1	1,502.4		
(Billion dollars)						

[a]Estimates for foreign assets were used where the data were missing.

Source: UNCTAD, Programme on Transnational Corporations (1993), p. 28.

to entail a disproportionate concentration of headquarters no matter what measure one uses. Third, different economic histories and business traditions may combine to produce different results.

Finally, headquarters concentration may be linked to a specific economic phase. For instance, unlike New York's loss of top Fortune 500 headquarters, Tokyo has been gaining these types of headquarters. Osaka and Nagoya, the two other major economic centers in Japan, are losing headquarters to sharp concentration in Tokyo. This change seems to be linked to the increasing internationalization of the Japanese economy and the corresponding increase in central command and servicing functions in Tokyo, Japan's major international business center. In the case of Japan, extensive government regulation over the economy is an added factor contributing to headquarters location in Tokyo because all international activities have to go through various government approvals (see Sassen, 1991, Chap. 1 and 7).

In brief, understanding the meaning of headquarters concentration requires differentiation along the variables just described. Although headquarters are still disproportionately concentrated in major cities, the patterns evident today do represent a change from 20 years ago.

The discussion about producer services, the producer services complex, and the locational patterns of headquarters points to two significant developments over the last 10 to 15 years. One is the growing service intensity in the organization of the economy, and the other, the emergence of a producer services complex which, although strongly geared toward the corporate sector, is far more likely to remain concentrated in urban centers than are the headquarters it serves.

The subject of the rise of the producer services complex inevitably brings up the financial and real estate crisis of the early 1990s, since so much of the highly speculative character of the 1980s was engineered by financial, legal, accounting, and other kindred experts in the major international business centers.

Impact of the Late 1980s Financial Crisis on Global City Functions: The Case of New York City

The high level of speculation and profitability that fed this growth in the 1980s was clearly unsustainable. The late 1980s financial crisis raises two possibilities. One is that it represents a true crisis of an economic system; the other, that it is instead a sharp readjustment to more sustainable levels of speculation and profitability. New York was the first of the major international financial centers to experience massive losses. Its post-1990 evolution may provide some useful insights into the interaction between crisis and readjustment in the dominant sector.

Employment in banking in the city fell from 169,000 in 1989 to 157,000 in 1991. Most of this loss (more than 10,000 jobs) was in domestic banking. It should also be noted that some of these losses were the result of the massive restructuring within the industry, including mergers among large domestic banks.

In the securities industry, an area that suffered some of the sharpest job losses in the last two years, New York City remains strong. It houses six of the top ten securities firms worldwide as of late 1990. City firms and their overseas affiliates acted as advisors for almost 80 percent of the value of all international mergers and acquisitions at the height of the financial boom in the mid-1980s. Because the securities industry is almost completely export oriented, it may well be less sensitive to the overall crisis in the U.S. economy and in New York City specifically. In terms of jobs, the largest branch of the industry is security brokers and dealers.

Even after the financial crisis of the last few years, New York City continues to function as an important international center and continues to be dominated by financial and related industries. According to many analysts, the crisis was a much needed adjustment to the excesses of the 1980s. Within the United States, New York City remains the banking capital of the country, leading in total assets, number of banks, and volume in various markets (currency, options trading, merchant banking).

Furthermore, foreign banking is a growth sector in New York City and may well be a key factor in the continuing role of the city as a leading financial center for the world. So, even as Japanese and European banks have far surpassed U.S. banks and dominate the international banking industry (see Table 2.2), all have offices in New York City. Indeed, in 1990, New York City surpassed London in its number of international bank offices. Notwithstanding reductions in the domestic banking industry and major crises in several industry branches, New York remains truly a platform for international operations.

What emerges from these developments is that New York City may retain its central role as a financial center but with a far greater participation by foreign firms making loans, selling financial services, and assisting in mergers and acquisitions. The job losses and bankruptcies in the securities industry since 1987 point to the possibility of a major transformation in the role of Wall Street and other stock markets, most particularly in that large corporations can bypass stock markets to raise investment capital. But drastic change does not spell the end of Wall Street. The crisis may prove to be partly a restructuring process from which Wall Street may emerge as a smaller market catering to smaller firms, but without losing an international base, and continuing as a provider of the most specialized and complex services.

Conclusion: Cities as Post-Industrial Production Sites

A central concern in this chapter was to look at cities as production sites for the leading service industries of our time, and hence to recover the infrastructure of activities of firms and jobs that is necessary to run the advanced corporate economy. Specialized services are usually understood in terms of specialized outputs rather than the production process involved. A focus on the production process allows us (1) to capture some of the locational characteristics of these service industries; and (2) to examine the proposition that there is a producer services complex which, although catering to corporations, has distinct locational and production characteristics. It is this producer services complex more so than headquarters of firms generally that benefits and often needs a city location. We see this dynamic for agglomeration operating at different levels of the urban hierarchy, from the global to the regional.

At the global level, a key dynamic explaining the place of major cities in the world economy is that they concentrate the infrastructure and the servicing that produce a capability for global control. The latter is essential if geographic dispersal of economic activity—whether factories, offices, or financial markets—is to take place under continued concentration of ownership and profit appropriation. This capability for global control cannot simply be subsumed under the structural aspects of the globalization of economic activity. It needs to be produced. It is insufficient to posit, or take for granted, the awesome power of large corporations.

By focusing on the production of this capability, we add a neglected dimension to the familiar issue of the power of large corporations. The emphasis shifts to the *practice* of global control: the work of producing and reproducing the organization and management of a global production system and a global marketplace for finance, both under conditions of economic concentration. Power is essential in the organization of the world economy, but so is production: the production of those inputs that constitute the capability for global control and the infrastructure of jobs involved in this production. This allows us to focus on cities and on the urban social order associated with these activities.

5

Issues and Case Studies in the New Urban Economy

Several of the questions raised in the preceding chapter can be fruitfully addressed through a closer look at cases of individual cities and issues of the new urban economy. The organizing focus of this chapter is the growing concentration and specialization of financial and service functions that lie at the heart of the new urban economy at a time when we might expect the development of global telecommunications to be pushing them toward geographic dispersal. These specific case studies provide insights into the dynamics of contemporary globalization processes as they materialize in specific places. They also present, in somewhat schematic form, a logic of inquiry into these issues that can be replicated in studies of other cities. Finally, we have chosen for our three case studies cities that are not among the absolute top tier, such as New York or Tokyo, but are lesser-known, smaller cities that we do not usually think of as being sites for global processes.

We begin with an examination of the formation of global city functions. We have chosen Miami to illustrate this process because we can see there, in incipient form, the implantation of the growth dynamic described in Chapter 4. The question here is, Under what conditions do global city functions materialize? Our second case study is Toronto, a city that built up its financial district only over the last few years and hence could have opted for far more dispersal than can old financial centers. Focusing on a broader, national geography, we chose Sydney in Australia to examine how these tendencies toward concentration operate in the case of a multipolar urban system and a vast, rich economy. Can we expect a similar multipolarity in the distribution of financial functions? After looking at these cities as laboratory cases, we examine the general trend toward concentration in financial and top-level service functions against a broader historical and geographic perspective. Is this a new trend? Is it likely to remain unchanged? Finally, we examine the question of urban form: What is the geographic correlate of the center, the terrain where the international financial and business center and the producer services complex materialize?

The Development of Global City Functions: The Case of Miami

Each of today's global cities has a specific history that has contributed to its current status. Many of the world's major cities enjoyed a long history as banking and trading centers or as capitals of commercial empires. This fact raises two immediate questions: What aspects of today's global cities are a continuation of past functions? How can global city functions emerge in cities that lack a long history as international banking and trading centers?

Miami is a case in point. On one hand, it is a city with a short history, one lacking any significant international functions. On the other hand, its large Cuban immigration led to the development in the 1960s and 1970s of an international trading complex oriented to Latin America and the Caribbean. The relative simplicity of Miami's history and of its international trading functions makes it relatively easy to disentangle two key processes: the continuity of the Cuban-led trading complex and the formation of a new business complex responding to the demands created by current processes of globalization. The case of Miami also helps us understand how a city can become a site for global city functions.

A growing number of U.S., European, and Asian firms have set up offices in Miami since the late 1980s. Miami now has the fourth largest concentration of foreign bank offices in the United States, right behind New York, Los Angeles, and Chicago and above San Francisco, Boston, or Atlanta. Eastman Kodak moved its headquarters for Latin American operations from Rochester in New York to Miami, and Hewlett-Packard made a similar move from Mexico City to Miami. Firms and banks from Germany, France, Italy, South Korea, Hong Kong, and Japan, to name but some, have all opened offices and brought in significant numbers of high-level personnel. Alongside these developments, there has been sharp growth in financial and specialized services for business. Miami's media image is so strongly associated with immigration and drugs that the formation of a new international corporate sector has not received much attention.

The scale of these developments leads us to ask whether Miami, although not quite a global city of the first rank, may have emerged as a site for global city functions. The case of Miami is also interesting because the city already has a concentration of international trading operations built and owned in good part by the prosperous resident Cuban elite (Portes & Stepick, 1993). Since their arrival in the 1960s after the 1959 Castro revolution, the Cuban community has built an impressive international trading entrepot, with a strong presence of firms and banks from Latin America and the Caribbean. Is the existence of the Cuban enclave, then, with its multiple trading operations for the Caribbean and Latin America, the base on which these new global city functions developed? Or is the latter a somewhat autonomous process that certainly may benefit from the concentration of trading operations in Miami but that responds to a different logic? Does it represent a type of development that would have taken place anyway in the southern Atlantic region (although perhaps not in Miami) had it not been for the Cuban enclave? In brief, what is the relation between these two processes, one shaped by past events and the other by the current demands of economic globalization?

Some of the hypotheses in the research literature on global cities are of interest here, especially those that examine the spatial and organizational forms assumed by economic globalization today and the actual work of running transnational economic operations. Figures on the growth of Miami's foreign banks, foreign headquarters, prime office-space market, installation of major telecommunications facilities, high-income residential and commercial gentrification, and high-priced international tourism all point to developments that transcend both the Cuban enclave and the Caribbean import/export enterprises in its midst. They point to another dynamic, one at least partly rooted in the new forms of economic globalization. They suggest that the growth of the new international corporate sector in Miami is part of this new dynamic rather than a mere expansion of the Latin American and Caribbean trading operations.

As described in Chapter 2, overall international business transactions with Latin America are growing rapidly. Total foreign direct investment in the newly opened Latin American economies grew from US$6.1 billion in 1984–87 to over $10 billion in 1988–89, $14 billion in 1991, and $16 billion in 1992. As we saw there, privatization, deregulation of stock markets and other financial markets, and the new export-oriented development model in most of Latin America are major factors. These are all extremely complicated transactions that require vast specialized inputs— a far cry from the earlier type of trading that initiated the growth of Miami in the 1970s.

One could argue that democratization and the opening of Latin American economies to foreign trade and investment should have made Miami less rather than more important. Yet, as we saw in Chapters 3 and 4, the evidence for many cities that function as international business centers shows sharp growth in the concentration of top-level managerial and specialized servicing activities. And it also points to a similar trend in Miami.

Over the last few years, Miami has also become a major administrative, managerial, and decision-making center. Since the mid-1980s the city has received a significant inflow of secondary headquarters. Large U.S. firms are reorganizing and expanding their Miami offices to handle new trade with Latin America. For example, Texaco's Miami office has increased its staff by 33 percent since 1987 to handle new operations in Colombia and Venezuela. And so has Miami's AT&T headquarters, which recently won 60 percent of a contract to upgrade Mexico's telecommunications infrastructure, which is no small job. Major companies such as France's Aerospatiale, Italy's Rimoldi, and Japan's Mitsui are opening operations in Miami. At the same time, Miami is a key platform for the operations of Latin American firms in the United States, and perhaps eventually even for operations with other Latin American countries. In addition, private investment in real estate, often for company housing by German, French, and Italian firms, has grown sharply in the last few years. Miami is beginning to concentrate transnational-level functions that used to be located in a variety of other areas. For instance, GM recently decided to relocate its headquarters for coordinating and managing Latin American operations from Sao Paulo in Brazil to Miami.

Miami also has significant international banking representation from Latin America, the Caribbean, Europe, and Asia. By 1992, Miami had 65 foreign bank offices. This is a small number compared with 464 in New York and 133 in Los Angeles, but it is not far from Chicago's 80 and makes Miami the fourth U.S. city in number of foreign bank offices. This is not insignificant if we consider that the ten top cities accounted for over 90 percent of all foreign bank offices in the United States, with New York City accounting for almost half. Almost all Miami offices were bank agencies and representative offices, both of which are full banking offices.

Miami is becoming a major telecommunications center for the region, which will further concentrate command functions there. For instance, AT&T has laid the first undersea fiber-optic cable to South America, connecting southern Florida to Puerto Rico, the Dominican Republic, Jamaica, and Colombia. The company is now working with Italy, Spain, and Mexico to build another fiber-optic link between those countries, the Caribbean, and Florida. Finally, we cannot overlook the significant concentration of telecommunication facilities associated with the large regional CIA headquarters, which can be of benefit, often indirectly, to commercial operations (Grosfoguel, 1993).

We can think of the Miami metropolitan area as a platform for international business transactions, a center for the long-distance coordination and management of transactions in Latin America and the Caribbean for firms from any part of the world interested in doing business in these regions.

The growing importance of these servicing and financing operations is reflected in the ascendance of these activities in the region's employment structure, the expansion of communications facilities, and the large supply of prime office space. It is not simply that employment in services grew by 46.3 percent from 1970 to 1990, partly as a function of population growth and general economic restructuring, but also that there has been a sharp recomposition in the components of services (Perez-Stable & Uriarte, 1993). In the recent past, domestic tourism and retail had been the driving growth sectors; by the late 1980s, it was finance and producer services, as well as new types of tourism—mostly international and high priced—and new types of retail—mostly upscale and catering to the expanded national and foreign corporate sector.

The key to the newly emergent Miami-area economy lies in the growth of producer services industries. Employment in these sectors almost doubled from 1970 to 1989 in Dade County, the Miami metropolitan area, reaching 20 percent of all private sector employment. Employment in banking and in credit agencies almost tripled. Business services more than doubled; so did specialized services, from engineering to accounting. The sharpest increase was the quadrupling in legal services employment. (Although part of the latter may be a result of the growth of Miami's other major industries, drugs and guns, at least some of it is linked to the growth of international finance and service functions.)

Industrial services are also a factor in these developments. Miami is a great transportation hub, with ports and airports that are among the busiest in the United States. The city's and its neighboring ports move more containerized cargo to Latin America than any other U.S. port. In terms of turnover of foreign passengers and cargo, Miami's airport is second only to New York City's Kennedy. In addition, the region now has a growing concentration of manufacturing firms aimed at the export market in the Caribbean and Latin America, as these areas become major buyers of U.S. goods. Miami's Free Trade Zone is one of the largest in the country.

All of this growth needs to be housed. At the end of the decade, Miami was in the top fifteen U.S. metropolitan areas in terms of prime rental office space supply. Though Miami's 44 million square feet are a fraction of top-listed New York City's 456.6 million square feet, it is not insignificant.

Why has this growth of a new international corporate sector taken place in Miami? Would these functions have been performed elsewhere had it not been for the Cuban enclave? The evidence suggests that the new international corporate sector responds to a different dynamic, one centered in the worldwide trend for firms to operate globally and on the growing importance and complexity of investment in Latin America. The growth of the Cuban enclave supported the internationalization of the city by creating a pool of bilingual managers and entrepreneurs skilled in international business. This resource gave the city an edge in the competition for the Latin trade. But is it sufficient to explain the subsequent agglomeration of U.S., European, and Asian corporate headquarters and bank offices and the sharp expansion in financial services?

The development of global city functions in Miami is centered on the recent sharp growth in the absolute levels of international investment in Latin America, the growing complexity of the transactions involved, and the worldwide trend for firms all over the world to operate globally. The Cuban enclave represents a significant set of resources, from international servicing know-how to Spanish-speaking personnel. But the particular forms of economic globalization evident over the last decade have implanted a growth dynamic in Miami that is distinct from the enclave, although benefiting from it. At the same time, although the new international corporate sector has made Miami a site for the transnational operations of firms from all over the world, these operations are still largely confined to Latin America and the Caribbean. In that sense we can think of Miami as a site for global city functions, although not a global city in the way that Paris or London is.

The Growing Density and Specialization of Functions in Financial Districts: Toronto

The leading financial districts in the world have all had rapid increases in the density of office buildings during the 1980s. There has also been a strong tendency toward growing specialization in the major activities housed in these buildings. It could be argued that one of the reasons for this continuing and growing concentration is that these are mostly old districts that have inherited an infrastructure built in an earlier, pre-telecommunications era, and hence they do not reflect a *necessary* form. In other words, the new density evident today would not be the result of agglomeration economies in the financial and corporate services complex, but rather would be an imposed form from the past.

The case of Toronto is interesting because so much of the city's financial district was built in the mid- to late 1980s, and it entered that decade with a far smaller and less prominent financial district than such cities as New York, London, or Amsterdam (City of Toronto, 1990). Furthermore, massive construction of office buildings also took place in the wider region around the city, including installation of all the most advanced communications facilities the 1980s offered. In terms of building and telecommunications technology, this might seem to be a case where much of the office infrastructure of the financial sector could have been located outside the small confines of the downtown. But that did not happen. According to Gunther Gad, a leading analyst of the spatial aspects of the office economy in Toronto, the demand was for a high-density office district; "'long walks' of 15 minutes are resented" (Gad, 1991, pp. 206–207; see also Canadian Urban Institute, 1993).

Initially Toronto's downtown office district housed manufacturing and wholesaling firms, the printing plants of the two main newspapers, and a large number of insurance firms. Much space was also allocated to retail; at one time there were street level shops and eating places on most blocks. Those were put underground, further raising the actual and visual office density of the district. Until the 1950s, the present financial district was still the general office district of the metropolitan area, containing the headquarters of firms in all major industries. Beginning at that time and continuing into the subsequent two decades, firms in a broad range of industries—insurance, publishing, architecture, engineering—moved out.

This is a pattern evident in other major cities: London saw a large number of its insurance headquarters move out; the downtowns of Frankfurt and Zurich became increasingly specialized financial districts; and New York saw the development of a new midtown office district that accommodated such growing industries as advertising and legal services, leaving Wall Street to become an increasingly specialized financial district.

Between 1970 and 1989, office employment in Toronto's financial district doubled, and its share of all employment rose from 77.6 percent to 92.3 percent, with a corresponding fall in nonoffice jobs. But the composition of office jobs also changed from 1970 and 1989, and the share of the insurance industry in all office activities fell from 14.6 percent to 9.8 percent, although it grew in absolute numbers. By 1989, well over half of all office employment was in finance, insurance, and real estate, and 28 percent in producer services. Gad (1991) found that banks, trust companies, investment services (including securities dealers), and real estate developers have grown strongly. Similarly, some of the producer services have grown very strongly: legal services, accounting, management consulting, and computer services. But others, such as architectural and engineering consulting, have not.

A more detailed analysis shows yet other patterns. Until the 1970s, it was typical for a large bank in a major city of a developed country to consolidate all its operations in one building in a city's financial district. By the early 1980s, it had become common for such institutions to relocate back-office jobs and branch functions out of the main office in the financial district to other parts of a city's larger metropolitan region. The same pattern was evident in Toronto. Spatial dispersal of more routine operations also took place within other industries—again, a pattern fairly typical for all major business centers. These trends, together with the growth in the share of high-level professional and managerial jobs, have led to an employment structure in Toronto's financial district that is highly bimodal, with 41 percent of all workers in top-level jobs—up from 31.5 percent in 1980—and about half of the jobs in clerical and other comparatively low-paying jobs.

Toronto has the largest concentration of corporate offices in Canada. Fifty of Canada's largest financial institutions are headquartered in Toronto, with 39 of them in the financial district. They include the majority of Canada's banks, foreign banks, and trust companies. Many other financial institutions have Toronto head-office subsidiaries, and some insurance companies located elsewhere have investment departments in Toronto. Here also are Canada's largest investment firms, several of the largest pension funds, and the various trade associations involved with finance and banking (Todd, 1993).

Generally it is top-level functions, and the most complex and innovative activities, that are carried out in the financial district of major cities. Routine operations can be moved outside the financial district. The more risk-laden, speculative activities, such as securities trading, have increased their share of activity in the financial district. The financial district is the place where large, complex loans can be put together; where complicated mergers and acquisitions can be executed; where large firms requiring massive investment capital for risky activities, such as real estate development or mining, can secure what they need, often combining several lenders and multiple lending strategies (Gad, 1991).

This is the specialized production process that takes place in the financial districts of today's major cities. It is the nature of these activities—the large amounts of capital, the complexity, the risk, and the multiplicity of firms involved in each transaction—that also contributes to the high density. On one hand, there is a built-in advantage in being located in a financial district where all the crucial players are located; on the other, the risk, complexity, and speculative character of much of this activity raises the importance of face-to-face interaction. The financial district offers multiple possibilities for face-to-face contact: breakfast meetings, lunches, inter- and intrafirm meetings, cocktail parties, and, most recently, health clubs. These are all opportunities for regularly meeting with many of the crucial individuals, for developing trust (of a specific sort) with potential partners in joint offerings; for making innovative proposals in terms of mergers and acquisitions or joint ventures. Telecommunications cannot replace these networks beyond the possibility of acting on new information obtained in a face-to-face encounter. The complexity, imperfect knowledge, high risk, and speculative character of many endeavors, as well as acceleration in the circulation of information and in the execution of transactions, heighten the importance both of personal contact and of spatial concentration. The case of Toronto suggests that the high density and specialization evident in all major financial districts is a response to the needs generated by current trends in the organization of the financial and related industries. Toronto could have built its financial sector on a more dispersed model, alongside the headquarters of the major national foreign firms that spread over its metropolitan area along hypermodern communications facilities. But it didn't, suggesting that the density of Toronto's downtown financial district is not the result of an inherited, old-fashioned built infrastructure, but a response to current economic requirements.

The Concentration of Functions and Geographic Scale: Sydney

The analysis of Toronto revealed two forms of concentration: One, the main focus of the section, was the disproportionate concentration of financial functions in one small district in the city. The other was the disproportionate concentration of all national financial and headquarter functions in Canada in a single city, Toronto. Are the tendencies toward concentration found in Toronto's financial district also evident when the geographic scale is the country, not the city—particularly for countries continental in scale and characterized historically by multiple-growth poles all oriented toward the world markets?

Here we want to examine in some detail this second tendency, toward concentration at the national scale, by focusing on Australia. Along with Canada and the United States, Australia has an urban system characterized by considerable multipolarity. This effect has been strengthened in Australia by the fact that it is an island-continent, which has promoted a strong outward orientation in each of its major cities. We might expect, accordingly, to find at work strong tendencies toward the emergence of several highly internationalized financial and business centers. Or, conversely, will we also see in Australia a space economy characterized by a disproportionate concentration of international business and financial functions in one city?

During the period from World War II to the 1970s, Australia became a very rich country with many large urban centers, thriving agricultural and manufacturing exports, and low unemployment. In the post–World War II period, Australia boasted several major urban areas and many growth poles. Melbourne, the old capital of the state of Victoria, had been and remained the traditional focus for commerce, banking, and headquarters, and generally the place of old wealth in Australia.

As did other developed economies, Australia experienced considerable restructuring beginning in the early 1970s: declines in manufacturing employment; growth in service employment; a shift to information-intensive industries; and a growing internationalization of production processes, services, and investment. In the mid-1980s, financial institutions were deregulated and integrated into global financial markets. There were massive increases in foreign direct investment, with a shift from agriculture, mining, and manufacturing to real estate and services and from European to Asian sources. Asian countries are now the main source of foreign investment in all major industries, and there generally is a greater orientation of trading and investment toward the Pacific rim (Daly & Stimson, 1992). Producer services emerged as the major growth sectors throughout all the metropolitan areas, and (combined with wholesale and retail and community services) accounted for 48 percent of all employment nationwide in Australia by the end of the 1980s. The fastest-growing export sectors were producer services and tourism.

The shift in investment in the 1980s from manufacturing to finance, real estate, and services became particularly evident in metropolitan areas (Stimson, 1993). It is in this conjunction that Sydney emerges as the major destination of investment in real estate and finance. In 1982–83 investment in manufacturing in Sydney was A$1.15 billion compared to A$1.32 billion in finance, real estate, and business services. By 1984–85 these levels of investment had changed, respectively, to A$0.82 billion and A\$1.49 billion. At lower levels, these trends were evident in other major urban areas (Stimson, 1993, p. 5). By 1986, however, there was a disproportionate concentration of finance and business services in Sydney that increasingly outdistanced other major cities. A massive real estate boom from 1985 to 1988 left Sydney the dominant market in Australia, both in levels of investment and in prime office space.

Sydney is Australia's main international gateway city and its only "world city," according to Daly and Stimson (1992). It has the largest concentration of international business and financial firms in Australia, having surpassed Melbourne, once the main economic capital of the country (see Table 5.1). About 150 international firms are headquartered in Sydney, compared to 43 in Melbourne. These represent 29 countries, including 48 firms from Japan, 29 from the United States, and 14 from the United Kingdom. Sydney has 10 commercial bank headquarters compared with 4 in Melbourne, and 81 in merchant banking compared to 6 in Melbourne. Sixty of Australia's largest 100 companies were headquartered in Sydney in 1989 compared with 45 in 1984; Melbourne had 29 in 1989 compared with 41 in 1984. Sydney's stock exchange is ranked ninth in the world in capitalization, its foreign exchange market is ranked eighth in turnover, and its futures exchange is the largest in the Asian region and the eighth largest in the world. Australia is emerging as an attractive location for secondary headquarters of Asian firms, and Sydney, where the majority of international contacts can be made, is by far the preferred city (O'Connor, 1990).

In its earlier phase, Australia had also been dependent on foreign investment to develop its manufacturing, mining, and agricultural sectors. But the share and order of magnitude of foreign investment in the 1980s

TABLE 5.1

Headquarters Concentration in Sydney and Melbourne, 1989

	Commercial Banks	Merchant Banks	International Firms	Top 100 Australian Corporations
Sydney	10	81	150	60 (45)[a]
Melbourne	4	6	43	29 (41)[a]

[a]Figures in parentheses are for 1984.

Source: Based on data from Stimson (1993).

point to a qualitative transformation and, in that sense, to a process of economic internationalization. From 1983–84 to 1988–89, foreign direct investment in Australia grew at an average of 34 percent a year, from A$81.9 billion to A$222.9 billion. Foreign investment in manufacturing also grew at a high rate, at 29 percent per year; but it grew at 83 percent a year in finance, real estate, and business services. This investment increasingly came from Japan and Asia, with declining shares coming from the United States and the United Kingdom (which were the two major investors in the past). Japan's share rose by 280 percent, reaching almost 15 percent of all foreign direct investment by 1989. Since 1990, Singapore, Hong Kong, and Taiwan have also become significant investors. In the second half of the 1980s, particularly following the deregulation of financial institutions, trading enterprises and banks were the major conduits through which capital entered the country. The real estate boom was directly linked to foreign investment, as was the real estate crisis of 1989–90, when foreign investors ceased pouring money into these markets. Over 28 percent of all FDI in 1985–86 went into real estate, growing to 46 percent by 1988–89. Japanese investors accounted for over a third of this investment. In that same period, 70 percent of investment proposals in tourism were Japanese. Investments to develop tourism rose from $A400 million in 1982 to A$1.61 billion in 1989; from 1987 to 1990 the value of major tourism projects either under construction or committed more than doubled to A$23 billion. This foreign investment was increasingly and disproportionately concentrated in New South Wales, which accounted for a third of all such investment, and in Queensland, with 21 percent; this represents a shift away from older regions such as Melbourne and its state of Victoria. Almost half of all investments in New South Wales, which has Sydney as its capital, were in commercial real estate.

The geography of these investments is made even more specific if we consider that the bulk of them were in the central business districts (CBDs) of major cities, with Sydney the leading recipient. Between 1975 and 1984, foreign investors had financed about 10 percent of total investment in commercial real estate; between 1980 and 1984 there were actually declines, reflecting the fall in global foreign investment in the early 1980s. But they picked up shortly after that, and by 1984, about 15 percent of CBD offices in Sydney were foreign-owned, and about 12.5 percent were in Melbourne (Adrian, 1984). In the second half of the 1980s there were sharp increases in investments in all CBDs of major cities, but especially in Sydney, Melbourne, and Brisbane. Stimson (1993) notes that by 1990 the value of land held by Japanese investors in Sydney's CBD was estimated at A\$1.55 billion, all of which had been invested in the second half of the 1980s. At the height of the boom in 1988–89, the officially estimated value of land in Sydney's CBD was put at \$A17.4 billion, a tenth of which was owned by Japanese investors.[1] Melbourne's CBD was also the object of much foreign investment acquisition, with record levels of construction in commercial real estate. In Brisbane, over 40 percent of the total office floor space was built between 1983 and 1990. Since those boom years, levels of foreign investment have fallen equally sharply, leaving a depressed office market in CBDs, a situation evident in major business centers all over the world.

It would seem, then, that even at the geographic scale and economic magnitude of a country like Australia, the ascendance of finance and services along with internationalization contribute to the marked concentration of strategic functions and investment in one city. Several experts on the Australian economy have noted that its increasing internationalization and the formation of new linkages connecting regions, sectors, and cities to the global economy have been central elements in the economic restructuring of that country (Daly & Stimson, 1992; O'Connor, 1990; Rimmer, 1988; Stimson, 1993). This process happened with great rapidity when we consider that not until 1983–84 did Australia deregulate its financial system, opening it up to world competition. Foreign investment patterns, international air passenger travel and tourism, and the location of activities and headquarters dependent on global networks all reflect this process of internationalization and concentration.

Globalization and Concentration: The Case of Leading Financial Centers

All the major economies in the developed world display a similar pattern of sharp concentration of financial activity and related producer services in one center: Paris in France, Milan in Italy, Zurich in Switzerland, Frankfurt in Germany, Toronto in Canada, Tokyo in Japan, Amsterdam in the Netherlands, and, as we have just seen, Sydney in Australia. The evidence also shows that the concentration of financial activity in such

---

[1]Japanese purchases of real estate have grown sharply. As recently as 1986 the value of such purchases stood at A\$119.5 million; by 1990 they had risen to A\$324 billion. The total value of Japanese acquisitions of real estate stood at A\$2.696 trillion by July 1990, already reflecting some devaluation due to the crisis beginning in 1989–90.

leading centers has actually increased over the last decade. Thus Basel, formerly a very important financial center in Switzerland, has now been completely overshadowed by Zurich (Keil & Ronneberger, 1993); and Montreal, certainly the other major center in Canada two decades ago, has now been overtaken by Toronto. Similarly, Osaka was once a far more powerful competitor with Tokyo in the financial markets in Japan than it was by the late 1980s (Sassen, 1991, Chap. 6 and 7).

Is this tendency toward concentration within each country a new development for financial centers? A broader historical view points to some interesting patterns. Since their earliest beginnings, financial functions were characterized by high levels of concentration. They often operated in the context of empires, such as the British or Dutch empires, or quasi-empires, such as the disproportionate economic and military power of the United States in the world over the last fifty years.

The first financial centers were medieval Italian cities such as Florence, a city with one of the most stable currencies in Europe, the florin. By the seventeenth century Amsterdam had taken over from these cities; it introduced central banking and the stock market, probably reflecting its vast international merchant and trading operations and Amsterdam's role as an unrivaled international center for trading and exchange. By 100 years later, London had emerged as the major international financial center and the major market for European government debt. London became the financial capital of the world clearly as a function of the British empire. By 1914 New York, which had won its competition with Philadelphia and Boston for the banking business in the United States, emerged as a challenger to London. London, however, was also the strategic cog in the international financial system, a role that New York was not quite ready to assume. But after World War II the immense economic might of the United States and the destruction of England and other European countries left New York the world's financial center.

Against this pattern of empires, the formation of nation-states represents a condition making possible a multiplicity of financial centers, typically the national capital in each country. Furthermore, the ascendance of mass manufacturing contributed to vast, typically regionally based fortunes and the formation of financial centers in those regions: Chicago and Osaka are only two examples. The renewed ascendance of finance in the 1980s, as we have seen, once again sharpened the tendencies toward concentration in a limited number of financial centers.

It would seem, then, that current developments are a continuation of an old pattern. We can begin to understand why, after a decade of massive growth in the absolute levels of financial activity worldwide, New

TABLE 5.2

International Bank Lending by Country
(percentage), 1980–1991

	1980	1991
United Kingdom	26.2	16.3
U.S.A.	9.4	9.4
France	9.4	6.6
Japan	6.2	15.1
Luxembourg	5.6	5.0
W. Germany	4.0	6.1[a]
Switzerland	3.4	6.3
Other	35.8	35.2
Total in US$ trillions	$1.89	$6.24

[a]Reunited Germany.

Source: Based on data from the Bank for International
Settlements, *62nd Annual Report* (Basel: B.I.S., 1992).

York, London, and Tokyo should remain in their position at the top and continue to account for such a disproportionate share of all activity. For example, international bank lending grew from US$1.89 trillion in 1980 to US$6.24 trillion in 1991—a threefold increase in a decade (see Table 5.2). New York, London, and Tokyo accounted for 42 percent of all such international lending in 1980 and for 41 percent in 1991, according to data from the Bank for International Settlements, the leading institution worldwide in charge of overseeing banking activity. There were compositional changes: Japan's share rose from 6.2 percent to 15.1 percent and the United Kingdom's fell from 26.2 percent to 16.3 percent; the U.S. share remained constant. All increased in absolute terms. Beyond these three, Switzerland, France, Germany, and Luxembourg bring the total share of the top centers to 64 percent in 1991, which is just about the same share these countries had in 1980. One city, Chicago, dominates the world's trading in futures, accounting for 60 percent of worldwide contracts in options and futures in 1991. Strong patterns of concentration are also evident in stock market capitalization and in foreign exchange markets (see Table 5.3).

We should note again that this unchanged level of concentration is in the context of enormous absolute increases, deregulation, and globaliza-

Foreign Exchange Turnover by Center:
Daily Averages, April 1989
(in US$ billions)

	Daily Turnover
London	190
New York	130
Tokyo	110
Zurich	55
Singapore	52
Hong Kong	50
Sydney	30
Paris	28

Source: Based on data from the Bank for International
Settlements, *62nd Annual Report* (Basel: B.I.S., 1992).

tion of the industry worldwide, which means that a growing number of
countries have become integrated into the world markets. Furthermore,
this unchanged level of concentration has happened at a time when financial services are more mobile than ever before: globalization, deregulation (an essential ingredient for globalization), and securitization have
been the key to this mobility, in the context of massive advances in telecommunications and electronic networks.[2] One result is growing competition among centers for hypermobile financial activity. In my view there
has been an overemphasis on competition in both general and specialized accounts on this subject. As Chapter 3 argued, there is also a func-
tional division of labor among various major financial centers. In that
sense we should also see at work here a system with multiple locations.

The hypermobility of financial capital puts added emphasis on the
importance of technology. It is now possible to move money from one
part of the world to another and make deals without ever leaving the
computer terminal. Thanks to electronics, there are now disembodied

---

[2]Securitization is the replacement of traditional bank finance by tradable debt;
for example, a mortgage is bundled up along with thousands of others into a
package that can be traded on specialized markets. This is one of the major
innovations in the financial industry in the 1980s. Securitization made it
possible to sell all kinds of (supposedly worthy) debt, thereby adding to the
overall volume of transactions in the industry.

marketplaces—what we can think of as the cyberspace of international finance (Sassen, 1993). NASDAQ (National Association of Securities Dealers Automated Quotations) and the foreign exchange markets, unlike the regular stock market with its trading floor, are examples of disembodied markets.

Yet the trend toward concentration still continues unabated—indeed, with renewed vigor—in the last decade. Furthermore, much of the discussion around the formation of a single European market and financial system has raised the possibility, and even the need, for a European financial system made competitive by centralizing financial functions and capital in a limited number of cities, rather than maintaining the current structure in which each country has a financial center.

These tendencies toward concentration seem to be built into the nature of such financial centers. Centers at the top are characterized by a multiplicity of financial institutions and markets and significant shares of world activity in various markets. They usually have a multiplicity of banks and other institutions that account for a significant share of international lending, foreign exchange trading, and fund management. They also have large or significant markets in tradable securities—whether bonds, stocks, or their derivatives.

Among the large financial centers, some are dominated by international business and others by domestic business. Thus London, with its strong Eurodollar markets and foreign exchange markets, is extremely international; whereas New York and Tokyo, with their enormous national economies, inevitably are going to have a very large incidence of domestic borrowers, lenders, and investors. The sharpest competition among the international financial centers is in the capital markets; some of the capital markets are extremely international, notably the foreign exchange and the Eurodollar markets. London has a very large share of these markets. Finally, the globalization of the industry has raised the level of complexity of transactions, and deregulation has promoted the invention of many new, complex instruments. This change clearly has raised the importance of the leading centers insofar as they are the only ones with the capability to handle such levels of complexity.

The Space Economy of the Center

What are the spatial consequences of this new economic core of activities? What is the urban form that accommodates them? Three distinct patterns are emerging in major cities and their regions in the developed countries. First, in the 1980s there was a growing density of workplaces in the traditional urban centers associated with growth in leading sectors and ancillary industries. This type of growth also took place in some of the most dynamic cities in developing countries, such as Bangkok, Taipei, Sao Paulo, Mexico City, and, toward the end of the decade, Buenos Aires. Second, along with this central city growth came the formation of dense nodes of commercial development and business activity in a broader urban region, a pattern not evident in developing countries except in the export-oriented growth poles discussed earlier. These nodes assumed different forms: suburban office complexes, **edge cities, exopoles,** urban agglomerations in peripheral areas. *Edge cities* refers to significant concentrations of offices and business activities alongside residential areas in peripheral areas that are completely connected to central locations via state-of-the-art electronic means. Thus far, these forms are only rarely evident in developing countries, where vast urban sprawl with a seemingly endless metropolitanization of the region around cities has been the norm. In developed countries, the revitalized urban center and the new regional nodes together constitute the spatial base for cities at the top of transnational hierarchies. The third pattern is the growing intensity in the "localness," or marginality, of areas and sectors that operate outside that world market–oriented subsystem, and this includes an increase in poverty and disadvantage. This general dynamic operates in cities with very diverse economic, political, social, and cultural arrangements. (See Benko & Dunford, 1991; Cheshire & Hay, 1989; Gans, 1984; Hausserman & Siebel, 1987; Henderson & Castells, 1987. See also Cobos, 1984.)

A few questions spring to mind. One question is whether the type of spatial organization characterized by dense strategic nodes spread over the broader region does or does not constitute a new form of organizing the territory of the "center," rather than, as in the more conventional view, an instance of suburbanization or geographic dispersal. Insofar as these various nodes are articulated through what I call cyberroutes or digital highways, they represent the new geographic correlate of the most advanced type of "center." The places that fall outside this new grid of digital highways are peripheralized. We might ask whether this is so now to a much higher degree than in earlier periods, when the suburban or noncentral economic terrain was integrated into the center because it was primarily geared *to* the center.

Another question is whether this new terrain of centrality is differentiated. Basically, is the old central city, which is still the largest and densest of all the nodes, the most strategic and powerful node? Does it have a sort of gravitational power over the region that makes the new grid of nodes and digital highways cohere as a complex spatial agglomeration? From a larger transnational perspective, these are vastly expanded central regions. This reconstitution of the center is different from agglomeration patterns still prevalent in most cities that have not seen a massive expansion in their role as sites for global city functions and the new regime of accumulation thereby entailed. We are seeing a reorganization of space/time dimensions of the urban economy.

It is under these conditions that the traditional perimeter of the city, a kind of periphery, unfolds its full industrial and structural growth potential. Commercial and office space development lead to a distinct form of decentralized reconcentration of economic activity on the urban periphery. This geographic shift has much to do with the locational decisions of transnational and national firms that make the urban peripheries the growth centers of the most dynamic industries.[3] It is distinctly not the same as largely residential suburbanization or metropolitanization.

We may be seeing a difference in the pattern of global city formation in parts of the United States and in parts of Western Europe. In the United States, major cities such as New York and Chicago have large centers that have been rebuilt many times, given the brutal neglect suffered by much urban infrastructure and the imposed obsolescence so characteristic of U.S. cities. This neglect and accelerated obsolescence produce vast spaces for rebuilding the center according to the requirements of whatever regime of urban accumulation or pattern of spatial organization of the urban economy prevails at a given time.

In Europe, urban centers are far more protected, and they rarely contain significant stretches of abandoned space; the expansion of workplaces and the need for "intelligent" buildings necessarily will have to take place partly outside the old centers. One of the most extreme cases is the complex of La Defense, the massive, state-of-the-art office complex developed right outside Paris to avoid harming the built environment inside the city. This is an explicit instance of government policy and planning aimed at addressing the growing demand for central office space of prime quality. Yet another variant of this expansion of the "center" onto hitherto peripheral land can be seen in London's Docklands. This vast and little-used harbor area in London became the site of an expensive, state-of-the-art development project that was meant to accommodate the

---

[3]That is, edge cities, exopoles, suburban office parks.

rapidly growing demand for office space in the center. The financial and real estate crisis of the early 1990s resulted in the collapse of the project. As of 1993, however, there has been a reorganization under a new consortium, and there is a rapidly growing interest on the part of worldwide buyers. Similar projects for recentralizing peripheral areas were launched in several major cities in Europe, North America, and Japan during the 1980s. What was once the suburban fringe, urban perimeter, or urban periphery has now become the site for intense commercial development.

Conclusion: Concentration and the Redefinition of the Center

The central concern in this chapter was to examine the fact of locational concentration of leading sectors in urban centers. This concentration has occurred in the face of globalization of economic activity, massive increases in the volume of transactions, and revolutionary changes in technology that neutralize distance.

A somewhat detailed empirical examination of several cases facilitated our understanding of different aspects of this trend toward concentration. Miami is a city that has emerged as a significant regional site for global city functions. What is interesting about Miami is that it lacks a long history as an international banking and business center, the typical case for such global cities as New York or London. Miami allows us to see in almost laboratory-like fashion how a new international corporate sector can become implanted in a site. It allows us to understand something about the dynamics of globalization in the current period and how it is embedded in place.

The case of Toronto, a city whose financial district was built up only in recent years, allows us to see to what extent the pressure toward concentration is embedded in an economic dynamic, and that it is not simply a consequence of a built infrastructure from the past, as one would expect in older centers such as London or New York. But Toronto also shows us that it is certain industries in particular that are subject to the pressure toward spatial concentration, most notably finance and its sister industries.

The case of Sydney allows us to explore the interaction of a vast, continental economic scale and pressures toward spatial concentration. Rather than strengthening the multipolarity of the Australian urban system, the developments of the 1980s—increased internationalization of the Australian economy; sharp increases in foreign investment; a strong shift toward finance, real estate, and producer services—all contributed to a greater concentration of major economic activities and actors in Sydney. This concentration included a declining share of such activities and actors in Melbourne, long the center of commercial activity and wealth in Australia.

Finally, we examined the case of the leading financial centers in the world today in order to see whether their concentration of financial activity had declined given globalization of the markets and immense increases in the global volume of transactions. We found that their levels of concentration remain unchanged in the face of massive transformations in the financial industry and in the technological infrastructure this industry depends on.

But what exactly is the center in the contemporary economy, which is characterized by growing use of electronic and telecommunication capability? The final section of the chapter examined the spatial correlate of the center and posited that today there is no longer a simple, straightforward relation between centrality and such geographic entities as the downtown or the central business district. In the past, and up to quite recently in fact, the center was synonymous with the downtown or the CBD. Today, it was argued here, the spatial correlate of the center can assume several geographic forms. It can be the CBD, as it still is largely in New York City, or it can extend into metropolitan areas in the form of a grid of nodes of intense business activity, as we see in Frankfurt.

Elsewhere (Sassen, 1991) I have argued that we are also seeing the formation of a transterritorial "center" constituted via digital highways and intense economic transactions; I argued that New York, London, and Tokyo could be seen as constituting such a transterritorial terrain of centrality *with regard to a specific complex of industries and activities.* At the limit we may see terrains of centrality that are disembodied, that lack any territorial correlate, that are in the electronically generated space we call cyberspace. As was argued in an earlier chapter, certain components of the financial industry, particularly the foreign currency markets, can be seen as operating partly in cyberspace.

One of the reasons for focusing on centrality and on its spatial correlates is to recover a particular kind of place—cities—in the operation of global processes. Such a recovery of place allows us to introduce questions concerning the social order associated with some of these transformations. This is the subject of the next chapter.

6

The New Inequalities within Cities

What is the impact of the ascendance of finance and producer services on the broader social and economic structure of major cities? And what are the consequences of the new urban economy on the earnings distribution of a city's workforce? We know that when manufacturing was the leading sector of the economy, it created the conditions for the expansion of a vast middle class because (1) it facilitated unionization; (2) it was based in good part on household consumption, and hence wage levels mattered in that they created an effective demand; and (3) the wage levels and social benefits typical of the leading sectors became a model for broader sectors of the economy.

We want to know about the place of workers lacking the high levels of education required by the advanced sectors of the economy in these major cities. Have these workers become superfluous? We also want to know about the place in an advanced urban economy of firms and sectors that appear to be backward or to lack the advanced technological and human capital base of the new leading sectors. Have they also become superfluous? Or are such workers, firms, and sectors actually articulated to the economic core, but under conditions of severe segmentation in the social, economic, racial, and organizational traits of firms and workers? We want to know, finally, to what extent this segmentation is produced or strengthened by the existence of ethnic/racial segmentation in combination with racism and discrimination.

Remarkably enough, we can see general tendencies at work on the social level just as we can on the economic level. Recent research shows sharp increases in socioeconomic and spatial inequalities within major cities of the developed world. This finding can be interpreted as merely a quantitative increase in the degree of inequality, one that is not associated with the emergence of new social forms or class realignments. But it can also be interpreted as social and economic restructuring and the emergence of new social forms: the growth of an informal economy in large cities in highly developed countries; high-income commercial and residential gentrification; and the sharp rise of homelessness in rich countries.

Our concern in this chapter is to describe the general outlines of this transformation. The nature of the subject is such that a fully adequate account would require introducing the specific conditions typical to each city, a task that falls outside the limits of this book. For that reason, too, much of the empirical background shaping some of the specific statements made here comes from the case of the United States. The reasons for focusing particularly on the United States are that there are more detailed analyses available and the trends under discussion are sharper.

The first half of the chapter discusses the transformation in the organization of the labor process, particularly as it materializes in large cities. The second half focuses on the earnings distribution in a service-dominated economy. This discussion includes somewhat more detailed accounts of the informal economy and of the restructuring of urban consumption, two key processes embedded in the changed earnings distribution.

Transformations in the Organization of the Labor Process

The consolidation of a new economic core of professional and servicing activities needs to be viewed alongside the general move to a service economy and the decline of manufacturing. New economic sectors are reshaping the job supply. So, however, are new ways of organizing work in both new and old sectors of the economy. The computer can now be used to do secretarial as well as manufacturing work. Components of the work process that even ten years ago took place on the shop floor and were classified as production jobs today have been replaced by a combination of machine/service worker or worker/engineer. The machine in this case is typically computerized; for instance, certain operations that required a highly skilled craftsperson can now be done through computer-aided design and calibration. Activities that were once consolidated in a single-service retail establishment have now been divided between a service delivery outlet and central headquarters. Finally, much work that was once standardized mass production is today increasingly characterized by customization, flexible specialization, networks of subcontractors, and informalization, even at times including sweatshops and industrial homework. In brief, the changes in the job supply evident in major cities are a function of new sectors as well as of the reorganization of work in both the new and the old sectors.

The historical forms assumed by economic growth in the post–World War II era that contributed to the vast expansion of a middle class—notably, capital intensity, standardized production, and suburbanization-led growth—deterred and reduced systemic tendencies toward inequality by constituting an economic regime centered on mass production and mass consumption. (Furthermore, so did the cultural forms accompanying these processes, particularly as they shaped the structures of everyday life insofar as a large middle class contributes to mass consumption and thus to standardization in production.) These various trends led to greater levels of unionization and other forms of workers' empowerment that can be derived from large scales in production and the centrality of mass production and mass consumption in national economic growth and profits. This form of economic growth, along with government programs, contributed to reduce the number of poor in the United States (see Figure 6.1) and in most highly developed economies.

It was also in that postwar period extending into the late 1960s and early 1970s that the incorporation of workers into formal labor market relations reached its highest level in the most advanced economies. The formalization of the employment relation carries with it the implementation (albeit frequently precarious) of a set of regulations that have had the overall effect of protecting workers and securing the fruits of frequently violent labor struggles. (But this formalization also entailed the exclusion of distinct segments of the workforce, particularly in certain heavily unionized industries.)

FIGURE 6.1

The Number of Poor People in the United States, 1959–1989

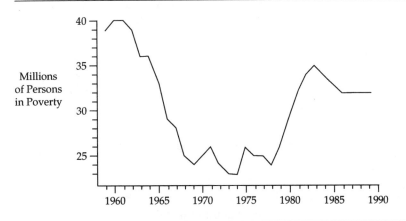

Source: Bureau of the Census, *Money Income and Poverty Status in the United States, 1989* (Washington, DC: U.S. Government Printing Office, 1989), Series P-60, No. 168, Table 19.

The economic and social transformations in the economy since the mid-1970s assume specific forms in urban labor markets. Changes in the functioning of urban labor markets since the mid-1970s have a number of possible origins. The most evident stems from the long-term shifts in the occupational and industrial balance of employment, which directly affects the mix of job characteristics, including earnings levels and employment stability, and the types of careers available to local workers. On the demand side, these developments include the new flexibility that employers have tended to seek under the pressure of international competition, unstable product markets, and a weakening of political support for public sector programs. This new flexibility tends to mean more part-time and temporary jobs. On the supply side, a key factor has been the persistence of high unemployment for over a decade in many large cities, which notably altered the bargaining position of employers, and the insecurity or marginalization of the most disadvantaged groups in the labor market. Workers desperate for jobs have been willing to take increasingly unattractive jobs. In combination, these major developments on the two sides of the labor market, all of which have operated most strongly in the urban core, seem likely to have induced, on the one hand, a growing destabilization of employment with increasing casualization and/or informalization of jobs and, on the other hand, an increasing polarization of employment opportunities with new types of social divisions.

Metropolitan labor markets will tend to reflect a variety of background factors beyond particular restructuring effects. The most important include their sheer size and density, the particular industrial and occupational mix of their employment base, the overall state of tightness or slack in labor demand, and, in many cities, the presence and characteristics of immigrant groups. Two characteristics of the labor markets in major cities today (as well as a century ago) are the fluidity and openness that influence the types of activity prospering there, as well as the labor market experiences of their residents. But equally important is the fact that the labor markets in and around the cities are *structured* with particular sets of jobs having attached to them distinctive combinations of rewards, security, and conditions of access (see Gordon & Sassen, 1992).

The labor market characteristics of many important industries in major cities evidence tendencies toward shorter-term employment relationships. Whether it is fashion-oriented industries such as the garment trade, private consumer services, trades historically associated with mass production, or the current speculative financial services, a significant share of establishments operate in competitive and often highly unstable markets. Again the evidence is that turnover rates in these activities are much higher than in large establishments and in monopolistic, bureau-cratized organizations. And one of the attractions of cities for these more unstable activities must be the ease with which employment levels can be adjusted up and down because of their fluid labor markets.

High rates of turnover also have implications on the supply side, adding to the attractions of the city for speculative migrants, particularly for minorities who have difficulty gaining access to more closed sectors of employment and for young single workers for whom job security may be a lower priority. The availability of these particular labor supplies must then have further implications for employers' strategies. The actual structure of urban labor markets has been more complex and changeable than agglomeration economies and the "natural selection" of activities and groups of workers can account for. The rapid growth in unemploy-ment levels in many European cities captures the overall outcome of these various processes. The European case is particularly interesting be-cause it has a stronger tradition of government protection of workers (see Table 6.1).

The potential importance of the presence or absence of a large immi-grant labor force extends to a range of issues, including the level of wages in the lower part of the labor market and its implications for the cost of living and the competitiveness of local activities, as well as for patterns of segmentation and opportunities of advancement for indig-enous workers. Furthermore, given the typical concentration of new mi-grants in central cities, immigration has also contributed to changes in spatial patterns in labor supply. In the United States there has also been a marked decentralization of the white population into the outer rings of the metropolitan regions; in major cities, white flight to the suburbs was counterbalanced by mostly third-world immigration into urban centers from the mid-1970s on.

Trends toward concentration of immigrants and ethnic populations in the center are also evident in other major cities in the developed world, from the well-known case of London to the little-known one of Tokyo. Thus, in 1991 Greater London had 1.35 million residents, or 20 percent of the population, classified as ethnic minorities. Ethnic minorities were 25.7 percent of the population of Inner London and about 17 percent in Outer London. Some of London's inner boroughs have extremely high concen-trations: Brent about 45 percent, Newham over 42 percent, and Tower Hamlets over 35 percent. Thus we see here a very high degree of spatial segregation and heavy concentration in central urban areas.

In Tokyo, 250,000 foreigners were officialy registered in 1991. This figure is an understatement because it excludes the growing illegal

TABLE 6.1

Unemployment in Select European Cities,
1980 and 1990

City	Unemployment in 1980 (percentage)	Unemployment in 1990 (percentage)
Amsterdam	8.2	19.5 (1988)
Barcelona	15.5 (1981)	14.6 (1988)
Birmingham	15.0	10.3
Brussels	6.0	16.7 (1989)
Copenhagen	7.8	11.3 (1988)
Dortmund	5.7	11.9
Dublin	9.9	18.4 (1987)
Glasgow	8.0	15.0
Hamburg	3.2	11.2
Liverpool	16.0	20.0
Lyons	6.1	8.3
Madrid	12.0	12.5
Marseilles	12.2	18.1
Milan	5.5 (1981)	5.0 (1989)
Montpellier	6.8	10.3
Naples	14.5	23.0
Paris	7.0	8.4
Rennes	8.1	10.1
Rotterdam	8.8	17.1 (1988)
Seville	18.7	25.2
Valencia	9.9	17.5

Source: Based on *A Report to the Commission of the European
Communities, Directorate General for Regional Policy (XVI),* April
1992, pp. 83–87.

immigration (see Morita, 1993; Sassen, 1993). But also in Tokyo we see a
pattern of spatial concentration in the center of the city. Thus 85 percent
of these registered foreigners were living in central Tokyo. But a disproportionate share, especially those of Asian origin, are concentrated in a
few small areas in the center of the city. Although the registered foreign
population represents a mere 2.3 percent of the total population of central Tokyo, its share rises to 5 percent in the center of the city. As in London, this is right next to the general area that houses the financial

institutions and the headquarters of important Japanese and foreign firms (Sassen, 1991, Chap. 9); it is the national and international business and financial heart of the Japanese economy. Furthermore, in some of the areas in the inner city where Asians are concentrated—and, it is known, where many of the unregistered, undocumented new immigrants live—foreigners account for a much larger proportion of residents. In Shinjuku ward, the new site of the city's government and a major commercial center, there are sections where foreigners account for 15 to 20 percent of all residents: Kabukicho and Ohkubo are examples (Sonobe, 1993). About two-thirds of these foreigners are Korean and Chinese, but there are also rapidly growing numbers of foreigners from other Asian countries.

The expansion of low-wage jobs as a function of growth trends implies a reorganization of the capital/labor relation. To see this effect clearly, we must distinguish the *characteristics* of jobs from their sectoral location. That is, highly dynamic, technologically advanced growth sectors may well contain low-wage, dead-end jobs. Furthermore, the distinction between sectoral characteristics and sectoral growth patterns is crucial: backward sectors such as downgraded manufacturing or low-wage service occupations can be part of major growth trends in a highly developed economy. It is often assumed that backward sectors express decline trends. Similarly, there is a tendency to assume that advanced industries, such as finance, have mostly good, white-collar jobs when in fact they also have a significant share of low-paying jobs, from cleaners to stock clerks.

We tend to think of finance and specialized services as a matter of expertise rather than of production. High-level business services, from accounting to decision-making expertise, are not usually analyzed in terms of their production process. Thus insufficient attention has gone to the actual array of jobs from high-paying to low-paying that are involved in the production of these services. In fact, the elaboration of a financial instrument, for example, requires inputs from law, accounting, advertising, and other specialized services. Advanced services benefit from agglomeration and show a tendency toward forming a production complex, as was discussed in Chapter 4. The production process itself, moreover, includes a variety of workers and firms not usually thought of as part of the information economy—notably, secretaries, maintenance workers, and cleaners. These latter jobs are also key components of the service economy. Thus, no matter how high the place a city occupies in the new transnational hierarchies, it will have a significant share of low-wage jobs thought of as somewhat irrelevant in an advanced information economy, even though they are an integral component.

There have been objective transformations in the forms of organizing manufacturing, with a growing presence of small-batch production, small scales, high product differentiation, and rapid changes in output. These elements have promoted subcontracting and the use of flexible ways of organizing production. Flexible forms of production, ranging from highly sophisticated to very primitive, can be found equally in advanced or in backward industries. Such ways of organizing production assume distinct forms in the labor market, in the components of labor demand, and in the conditions under which labor is employed. Indications of these changes are the decline of unions in manufacturing, the loss of various contractual protections, and the increase of involuntary, part-time, and temporary work or other forms of contingent labor. An extreme indication of this downgrading is the growth of sweatshops and industrial homework.

The expansion of a downgraded manufacturing sector partly involves the same industries that used to have largely organized plants and reasonably well-paid jobs, but it replaces these with different forms of production and organization of the work process, such as piecework and industrial homework. But it also involves new kinds of activity associated with the new major growth trends. The possibility for manufacturers to develop alternatives to the organized factory becomes particularly significant in growth sectors. The consolidation of a downgraded manufacturing sector—whether through social or technical transformation—can be seen as a politico-economic response to a need for expanded production in a situation of growing average wages and militancy (as was the case in the 1960s and early 1970s).

The Informal Economy

A good part of the downgraded manufacturing sector is an instance of **informalization**, or a component of the informal sector. Although informal sectors are thought to emerge only in third-world cities, we are now seeing rapid growth of informal work in most major cities in highly developed countries, from New York and Los Angeles to Paris and Amsterdam (Portes, Castells, & Benton, 1989; Renooy, 1984; WIACT, 1993).

We need to distinguish two spheres for the circulation of goods and services produced in the informal economy. One sphere circulates internally and mostly meets the demands of its members, such as small immigrant-owned shops in the immigrant community that service the latter; the other circulates throughout the "formal" sector of the economy. In this second sphere, informalization represents a direct profit-maximizing strategy, one that can operate through subcontracting, the use of sweatshops and homework, or direct acquisition of goods or services. We are seeing not only increasingly downgraded manufacturing but also downgraded mass consumer services, whether public or private, alongside increasingly upgraded non–mass consumer services.

These conditions suggest that the combination of several trends that are particularly evident in major cities present inducements to informalization: (1) the increased demand for highly priced customized services and products by the expanding high-income population; (2) the increased demand for extremely low-cost services and products by the expanding low-income population; (3) the demand for customized services and goods or limited runs from firms that are either final or intermediate buyers with a corresponding growth of subcontracting; (4) the increasing inequality in the bidding power of firms in a context of acute pressures on land because of the rapid growth and strong agglomerative pattern of the leading industries; and (5) the continuing demand by various firms and sectors of the population—including demand from leading industries and high-income workers—for goods and services typically produced in firms with low profit rates that find it increasingly difficult to survive aboveground, given rising rents and production costs.

The transformation of final and intermediate consumption and the growing inequality in the bidding power of firms and households create inducements for informalization in a broad range of activities and spheres of the economy. The existence of an informal economy in turn emerges as a mechanism for reducing costs, even in the case of firms and households that do not need it for survival, and for providing flexibility in instances where this is essential or advantageous.

The Earnings Distribution in a Service-Dominated Economy

What we want to know next is the impact that the shifts have had on the earnings distribution and income structure in a service-dominated economy. A growing body of studies on the occupational and earnings distribution in service industries finds that services produce a larger share of low-wage jobs than manufacturing does, although the latter may increasingly be approaching parity with services; moreover, several major service industries also produce a larger share of jobs in the highest-paid occupations (Goldsmith & Blakely, 1992; Harrison & Bluestone,

1988; Nelson & Lorence, 1985; Sheets, Nord, & Phelps 1987; Silver, 1984; Stanback & Noyelle, 1982).

Much scholarly attention has been focused on the importance of manufacturing in reducing income inequality in the 1950s and 1960s (Blumberg, 1981; Stanback et al., 1981). Central reasons typically identified for this effect are the greater productivity and higher levels of unionization found in manufacturing. Clearly, however, these studies tend to cover a period largely characterized by such conditions, and since that time the organization of jobs in manufacturing has undergone pronounced transformation. In what is at this point the most detailed analysis of occupational and industry data, Harrison and Bluestone (1988) found that earnings in manufacturing have declined in many industries and occupations. Glickman and Glasmeier (1989) found that a majority of manufacturing jobs in the sunbelt are low wage, and Fernandez-Kelly and Sassen (1992) found growth of sweatshops and homework in several industry branches in New York and Los Angeles.

There is now a considerable number of studies with a strong theoretical bent (Hill, 1989; Lipietz, 1988; Massey, 1984; Sassen, 1988; Scott & Storper, 1986) which argue that the declining centrality of mass production in national growth and the shift to services as the leading economic sector contributed to the demise of a broader set of arrangements. In the postwar period, the economy functioned according to a dynamic that transmitted the benefits accruing to the core manufacturing industries onto more peripheral sectors of the economy. The benefits of price and market stability and increases in productivity could be transferred to a secondary set of firms, including suppliers and subcontractors, but also to less directly related industries. Although there was still a vast array of firms and workers that did not benefit from the shadow effect, their number was probably at a minimum in the postwar period. By the early 1980s the wage-setting power of leading manufacturing industries and this shadow effect had eroded significantly (see Figures 6.2 and 6.3).

Scholarship on the impact of services on the income structure of cities is only now beginning to emerge in most countries. There are now several detailed analyses of the social impact of service growth in major metropolitan areas in the United States (Fainstein et al., 1986; Nelson & Lorence, 1985; Ross & Trachte, 1983; Sheets, Nord, & Phelps, 1987; Silver, 1984; Stanback & Noyelle, 1982). Sheets, Nord, and Phelps (1987) found that from 1970 to 1980 several service industries had a significant effect on the growth of underemployment, a label they define as employment paying below poverty-level wages in the 199 largest metropolitan areas. The strongest effect was associated with the growth of producer services

FIGURE 6.2

Rate of Change in Family Real Income, Quintiles, 1973–1989

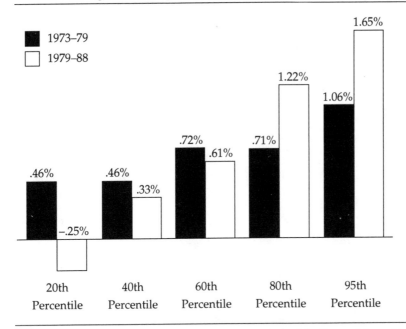

Legend:
■ 1973–79
□ 1979–88

Percentile	1973–79	1979–88
20th	.46%	-.25%
40th	.46%	.33%
60th	.72%	.61%
80th	.71%	1.22%
95th	1.06%	1.65%

Source: Goldsmith and Blakely, 1992, p. 22. Based on Bureau of the Census, Money Income and Poverty Status in the United States (Washington, DC: U. S. Government Printing Office, 1989), Series P-60, No. 168, Table 5; No. 129, Table 14; No. 97, Table 22; and Gary Burtless, "Trends in the Distribution of Earnings and Family Income," testimony before the Senate Budget Committee, Feb. 22, 1991.

and retail trade. The highest relative contribution resulted from what the authors call "corporate services" (FIRE, business services, legal services, membership organizations, and professional services), such that a 1 percent increase in employment in these services was found to result in a 0.37 percent increase in full-time, year-round, low-wage jobs. Furthermore, a 1 percent increase in distributive services resulted in a 0.32 percent increase in full-time, year-round, low-wage jobs. In contrast, a 1 percent increase in personal services was found to result in a 0.13 percent increase in such full-time jobs and a higher share of part-time, low-wage jobs. The retail industry had the highest effect on the creation of part-time, year-round, low-wage jobs, such that a 1 percent increase in retail employment was found to result in a 0.88 percent increase in such jobs.

FIGURE 6.3

Change in Average Real Hourly and Weekly Wages, 1970–1990 (in constant 1990 dollars)

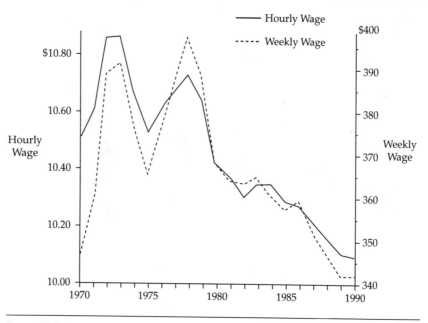

Source: U. S. Congress, House Committee on Ways and Means, Overview of Entitlement Programs: Green Book, 1991, Appendix F, Table 34.

But what about the impact of services on the expansion of high-income jobs? Nelson and Lorence (1985) examined this question using census data on the 125 largest urban areas. To establish why male earnings are more unequal in metropolises with high levels of service sector employment, they measured the ratio of median earnings over the 5th percentile to identify the difference in earnings between the least affluent and the median metropolitan male earners; and they measured the ratio at the 95th percentile to establish the gap between median and affluent earners. Overall, they found that inequality in the 125 areas appeared to be the result of greater earnings disparity between the highest and the median earners than between the median and lowest earners (Nelson & Lorence, 1985, p. 115). Furthermore, they found that the strongest effect came from the producer services and that the next strongest was far weaker (social services in 1970 and personal services in 1980).

The conditions for ongoing inequality can also be seen in projections for educational requirements. In the United States, the evidence for 1988 shows that 17 percent of jobs required less than a high school diploma and over 40 percent would require only a high school diploma. Only about 22 percent of jobs required at least a college degree. By the year 2000 the expectation is that there will be very little change in these levels, with 16.5 percent of jobs requiring less than high school and only 22.9 percent requiring at least a college degree. That is to say, by the year 2000 over half of all jobs will require only a high school diploma or less. The change is somewhat sharper when we consider only net new jobs, with only 13 percent of jobs requiring less than high school and almost 30 percent requiring at least a college degree (Bailey, 1990). The expansion of low-wage service jobs in large cities and the downgrading of many manufacturing jobs suggest that a good share of jobs in cities will be among those requiring only a high school education or less.

In their own distinct form, these trends are evident in many highly developed countries (Brosnan & Wilkinson, 1987; Cheshire & Hay, 1989; Mingione, 1991). Of interest here is Japan, since little seems to be known or reported in general commentary about growing casualization of employment. We now turn to a brief description of the growth of service jobs in Japan.

The Growth of Low-Wage Jobs in Japan

Japan also has seen considerable growth of low-wage service jobs, the replacement of many full-time male workers with part-time female workers, and the growth of forms of subcontracting that weaken the claims of workers on their firms. Over half of the new jobs created in Tokyo in the 1980s were part-time or temporary jobs.

There are other indications of structural change in Japan in the 1980s. Since the mid-1980s, average real earnings in Japan have been decreasing, and the manufacturing sector has been losing its wage-setting influence. Furthermore, with few exceptions, most of the service industries that *are* growing have significantly lower average earnings than do manufacturing, transport, and communications. Hotel and catering had among the lowest average earnings, along with health services and retail. Many of the industries that are growing either pay above-average wages—as in finance, insurance, and real estate—or pay below-average wages. The same trends found in many western cities are becoming evident in Tokyo. (For a full discussion, see Sassen, 1991, Chap. 8 and 9).

Data from the Labor Force Survey in Japan show that the share of part-time workers increased from under 7 percent of all workers in 1970 to 12 percent in 1987, or 5 million workers. Among female workers, this share almost doubled, from about 12 percent in 1970 to 22 percent in 1985 and over 23 percent in 1987, or a total of about 3.65 million women.[1] Almost 24 percent of part-time female workers were in manufacturing, an indication of the growth of a casualized employment relation in that sector.

By the late 1980s, 58 percent of all firms surveyed employed part-time workers. Part-time work in Japan is defined by the Ministry of Labor as a job with scheduled hours per week "substantially shorter than those of regular workers." Part-time work is measured as regular employment of under thirty-five hours a week. This definiton excludes seasonal and temporary employment and is thus an undercount of all jobs that are not year-round, full-time jobs. What distinguishes them is the lack of various benefits and entitlements, or, in the terms used here, a casualized employment relation.

Of interest also is the situation of homeworkers, a growing category in most developed countries. Official counts of legal homeworkers in Japan show gradual decline over the last decade. In 1987 there were over 1 million such workers, almost all women (Japan Ministry of Labor, 1987). The largest share of homework, 34 percent, is in clothing and related items, followed by 18.6 percent in electrical/electronic equipment (including assembly of electronic parts) and almost 16 percent in textiles. The remaining share includes a very broad range of activities, from making toys and lacquerware to printing and related work. It is quite possible that the existing regulations protecting homeworkers and providing them with fringe benefits are eroding. Official figures describe a decline in the fully entitled share of homeworkers but possibly do not register an absolute increase among homeworkers with no protection. There are some indications that the latter category may be increasing (Sassen, 1991, Chap. 9).

The growth of low-wage and part-time jobs is likely to facilitate the employment of illegal immigrants. In Japan, where immigration, both legal and illegal, is not part of the cultural heritage as it is in the United States, there is now a growing illegal immigration from several Asian countries. The evidence on detected illegal immigrants from the Ministry of Justice analyzed by Morita (1992) shows that over 80 percent of

---

[1]All these figures exclude people employed in agriculture and forestry. Of 3.6 million female part-time workers, about 0.8 million were in manufacturing; 1.3 million in wholesale and retail trade; 170,000 in FIRE; and almost 1 million in service industries. (See Sassen, 1991.)

men apprehended from 1987 to 1990 held construction and factory jobs. Clearly, factories and construction sites lend themselves to apprehension activity, unlike small service operations in the center of Tokyo or Osaka. Thus we cannot assume that this level is an adequate representation of the occupational distribution of illegal immigrants; but it does indicate that factories are employing illegal immigrants.

According to a study of illegal immigrant employment in the major urban areas in Japan carried out by the Immigration Office of the Ministry of Justice, factories employing illegal immigrants are in a broad range of branches: metal processing, plastic processing, printing and binding, plating, press operating, materials coating. Most recently a growing number of women have been apprehended in factories in metals and plastic processing and in auto-parts manufacturing (Morita, 1990). Most illegal immigrants were found in medium-size and small factories. The figures for 1991 point to a continuation of these patterns; almost half of illegals detected by the government were in construction, followed by 14 percent in manufacturing and certain jobs in the retail industry, in particular back-room jobs in restaurants.

Estimates about the evolution of illegal immigration for unskilled jobs vary considerably, but all point to growing demand. The Ministry of Labor estimates the labor shortage will reach half a million by the end of the decade. Japan's most powerful business organization, Keidaren, puts the shortage at 5 million. Specialists estimate the shortage will range between 1 and 2 million by the end of the decade. Currently the largest shortages are in manufacturing, particularly small- and medium-size firms. But there is considerable agreement that the service sector will be a major source of new shortages. As the current generation of Japanese employees in low-skill service jobs retires and young highly educated Japanese reject these jobs, there may well be a gradual acceptance of immigrant workers. Although later than most advanced economies, Japan now has a growing labor demand for low-wage, unskilled jobs in a context where Japanese youth are rejecting such jobs.

The Restructuring of Urban Consumption

The rapid growth of industries with a strong concentration of high- and low-income jobs has assumed distinct forms in the consumption structure, which in turn has a feedback effect on the organization of work and the types of jobs being created. In the United States, the expansion of the high-income workforce in conjunction with the emergence of new cultural forms has led to a process of high-income gentrification that rests, in the last analysis, on the availability of a vast supply of low-wage workers. As I have argued at great length elsewhere, high-income gentrification is labor intensive, in contrast to the typical middle-class suburb that represents a capital-intensive process: tract housing, road and highway construction, dependence on private automobiles or commuter trains, marked reliance on appliances and household equipment of all sorts, large shopping malls with self-service operations. Directly and indirectly, high-income gentrification replaces much of this capital intensity with workers. Similarly, high-income residents in the city depend to a much larger extent on hired maintenance staff than does the middle-class suburban home, with its concentrated input of family labor and machinery.

Although far less dramatic than in large cities in the United States, the elements of these patterns are also evident in many major Western European cities and, to some extent, in Tokyo. For instance, there has been considerable change in the occupational composition of residents in central Tokyo. Not unlike what we have seen in other major cities, there is a tendency for growing numbers of upper-level professional workers and of low-level workers to live in central cities: Sonobe (1993) found that the share of the former grew from 20 percent of all workers in 1975 to over 23 percent in 1985 and (although difficult to measure) we know that the numbers of low-wage legal and undocumented immigrants also grew and certainly have grown sharply since then. The share of middle-level workers, on the other hand, fell: for instance, the share of skilled workers fell from 16 percent in 1975 to 12 percent in 1985. Similar patterns holds for other areas of the city (Sonobe, 1993). The total size of the resident workforce stayed the same, at about 4.3 million in 1975 and in 1985. We know that there was a sharp growth of high-income professional and managerial jobs in the second half of the 1980s, which could only have reinforced this trend.

The growth of the high-income population in the resident and commuting workforce has contributed to changes in the organization of the production and delivery of consumer goods and services. Behind the delicatessens and specialty boutiques that have replaced many self-service supermarkets and department stores lies a very different organization of work from that prevalent in large, standardized establishments. This difference in the organization of work is evident both in the retail and in the production phase (Gershuny & Miles, 1983; Sassen-Koob, 1984). High-income gentrification generates a demand for goods and services that are frequently not mass-produced or sold through mass outlets. Customized production, small runs, specialty items, and fine food dishes are generally produced through labor-intensive methods and sold through small, full-service outlets. Subcontracting part of this production to low-cost operations and to sweatshops or households is common. The overall outcome for the job supply and the range of firms involved in this production and delivery is rather different from that characterizing the large department stores and supermarkets. There mass production is prevalent, and hence large standardized factories located outside of the region are the norm. Proximity to stores is of far greater importance with customized producers. Mass production and mass distribution outlets facilitate unionizing. (See Sayer & Walker, 1992.)

The magnitude of the expansion of high-income workers and the high levels of spending contribute to this outcome. All major cities have long had a core of wealthy residents or commuters. By itself, however, this core of wealthy people could not have created the large-scale residential and commercial gentrification in the city. As a stratum, the new high-income workers are to be distinguished from this core of wealthy or upper class. The former's disposable income is generally not enough to make them into major investors. It is, however, sufficient for a significant expansion in the demand for highly priced goods and services— that is, to create a sufficiently large demand so as to ensure economic viability for the producers and providers of such goods and services. Furthermore, the level of disposable income is also a function of life-style and demographic patterns, such as postponing having children and larger numbers of two-earner households.

The expansion in the low-income population has also contributed to the proliferation of small operations and the move away from large-scale standardized factories and large chain stores for low-price goods. In good part, the consumption needs of the low-income population are met by manufacturing and retail establishments that are small, rely on family labor, and often fall below minimum safety and health standards. Cheap, locally produced sweatshop garments, for example, can compete with low-cost Asian imports. A growing number of products and services ranging from low-cost furniture made in basements to "gypsy cabs" and family daycare is available to meet the demand for the growing low-income population. (See Renooy, 1984.)

There are numerous instances of how the increased inequality in earnings reshapes the consumption structure and how this reshaping in turn has feedback effects on the organization of work. Some examples are the creation of a special taxi line for Wall Street that services only the financial district and an increase of "gypsy" cabs in low-income neighborhoods not serviced by regular cabs; the increase in highly customized woodwork in gentrified areas and low-cost rehabilitation in poor neighborhoods; the increase of homeworkers and sweatshops making either very expensive designer items for boutiques or very cheap products.

Conclusion: A Widening Gap

Developments in cities cannot be understood in isolation from fundamental changes in the larger organization of advanced economies. The combination of economic, political, and technical forces that has contributed to the decline of mass production as the central driving element in the economy brought about a decline in a broader institutional framework that shaped the employment relation. The group of service industries that constitute the driving economic force in the 1980s and into the 1990s is characterized by greater earnings and occupational dispersion, weak unions, and a growing share of unsheltered jobs in the lower-paying echelons, along with a growing share of high-income jobs. The associated institutional framework shaping the employment relation diverges from the earlier one. This new framework contributes to a reshaping of the sphere of social reproduction and consumption, which in turn has a feedback effect on economic organization and earnings. Whereas in the earlier period this feedback effect contributed to reproduction of the middle class, currently it reproduces growing earnings disparity, labor market casualization, and consumption restructuring.

All these trends are operating in major cities, in many cases with greater intensity than in medium-size towns. This greater intensity can be rooted in at least three conditions. First is the locational concentration of major growth sectors with either sharp earnings dispersion or disproportionate concentration of either low- or high-paying jobs. Second is a proliferation of small, low-cost service operations made possible by the massive concentration of people in such cites, in addition to a large daily inflow of nonresident workers and tourists. The ratio between the number of these service operations and the resident population is probably significantly higher in a very large city than in an average city. Furthermore, the large concentration of people in major cities tends to create intense inducements to open up such operations, as well as intense competition and very marginal returns. Under such conditions, the cost of labor is crucial, and hence the likelihood of a high concentration of low-wage jobs increases. Third, for these same reasons together with other components of demand, the relative size of the downgraded manufacturing sector and the informal economy would tend to be larger in big cities like New York or Los Angeles than in average-size cities.

The overall result is a tendency toward increased economic polarization. When we speak of polarization in the use of land, in the organization of labor markets, in the housing market, and in the consumption structure, we do not necessarily mean that the middle class is disappearing. We are rather referring to a dynamic whereby growth contributes to inequality rather than to expansion of the middle class, as was the case in the two decades after World War II in the United States and the United Kingdom, and into the 1970s in Japan. In many of these cities the middle class represents a significant share of the population and hence represents an important channel through which income and life-style coalesce into a social form.

The middle class in the United States is a very broad category. It contains prosperous segments of various ethnic populations in large cities as well as longtime natives. What we can detect in the 1980s is that certain segments of the middle class gain income and earnings, becoming wealthier while others become poorer. In brief, we see a segmenting of the middle class that has a sharper upward and downward slant than has been the case in other periods. The argument put forth here is that while the middle strata still constitute the majority, the conditions that contributed to their expansion and politico-economic power—the centrality of mass production and mass consumption in economic growth and profit realization—have been displaced by new sources of growth. This is not simply a quantitative transformation; we see here the elements for a new economic regime.

The growth of service employment in cities and the evidence of the associated growth of inequality raises questions about how fundamental a change this shift entails. Several of these questions concern the nature of service-based urban economies. The observed changes in the occupational and earnings distribution are outcomes not only of industrial shifts but also of changes in the organization of firms and of labor markets. A detailed analysis of service-based urban economies shows that there is considerable articulation of firms, sectors, and workers who may appear to have little connection to an urban economy dominated by finance and specialized services but in fact fulfill a series of functions that are an integral part of that economy. They do so, however, under conditions of sharp social, earnings, and often racial/ethnic segmentation.

7

A New Geography of Centers and Margins: Summary and Implications

Three important developments over the last 20 years laid the foundation for the analysis of cities in the world economy presented in this book. They are captured in the three broad propositions organizing the preceding chapters.

1. *The territorial dispersal of economic activities, of which globalization is one form, contributes to the growth of centralized functions and operations.* We find here a new logic for agglomeration and key conditions for the renewed centrality of cities in advanced economies. Information technologies, often thought of as neutralizing geography, actually contribute to spatial concentration. They make possible the geographic dispersal and simultaneous integration of many activities. But the particular conditions under which such facilities are available have promoted centralization of the most advanced users in the most advanced telecommunications centers. We see parallel developments in cities that function as regional nodes—that is, at smaller geographic scales and lower levels of complexity than global cities.

2. *Centralized control and management over a geographically dispersed array of economic operations does not come about inevitably as part of a "world system."* It requires the production of a vast range of highly specialized services, telecommunications infrastructure, and industrial services. Major cities are centers for the servicing and financing of international trade, investment, and headquarters operations. And in this sense they are strategic production sites for today's leading economic sectors. This function is reflected in the ascendance of these activities in their economies. Again, cities that serve as regional centers exhibit similar developments. This is the way in which the spatial effects of the growing service intensity in the organization of all industries materialize in cities.

3. *Economic globalization has contributed to a new geography of centrality and marginality.* This new geography assumes many forms and

operates in many terrains, from the distribution of telecommunications facilities to the structure of the economy and of employment. Global cities become the sites of immense concentrations of economic power, while cities that were once major manufacturing centers suffer inordinate declines; highly educated workers see their incomes rise to unusually high levels, while low- or medium-skilled workers see theirs sink. Financial services produce superprofits while industrial services barely survive.

Let us look more closely now at this last and most encompassing of the propositions.

The Locus of the Peripheral

The sharpening distance between the extremes evident in all major cities of developed countries raises questions about the notion of "rich" countries and "rich" cities. It suggests that the geography of centrality and marginality, which in the past was seen in terms of the duality of highly developed and less developed countries, is now also evident within developed countries and especially within their major cities.

One line of theorization posits that the intensified inequalities described in the preceding chapters represent a transformation in the geography of center and periphery. They signal that peripheralization processes are occurring inside areas that were once conceived of as "core" areas—whether at the global, regional, or urban level—and that alongside the sharpening of peripheralization processes, centrality has also become sharper at all three levels.

The condition of being peripheral is installed in different geographic terrains depending on the prevailing economic dynamic. We see new forms of peripheralization at the center of major cities in developed countries not far from some of the most expensive commercial land in the world: "inner cities" are evident not only in the United States and large European cities, but also now in Tokyo (Nakabayashi, 1987; Komori, 1983; KUPI, 1981; Sassen, 1991, Chap. 9). Furthermore, we can see peripheralization operating at the center in organizational terms as well (Sassen-Koob, 1980; Wilson, 1987). We have long known about segmented labor markets, but the manufacturing decline and the kind of devaluing of nonprofessional workers in leading industries that we see today in these cities go beyond segmentation and in fact represent an instance of peripheralization.

Furthermore, the new forms of growth evident at the urban perimeter also mean crisis: violence in the immigrant ghetto of the *banlieus* (the French term for *suburbs*), exurbanites clamoring for control over growth to protect their environment, new forms of urban governance (Body-Gendrot, 1993; Pickvance & Preteceille, 1991). The regional mode of regulation in many of these cities is based on the old center/suburb model and may hence become increasingly inadequate to deal with intraperipheral conflicts—conflicts among different types of constituencies at the urban perimeter or urban region. Frankfurt, for example, is a city that cannot function without its region's towns; yet this particular *urban region* would not have emerged without the specific forms of growth in Frankfurt's center. Keil and Ronneberger (1993) note the ideological motivation in the call by politicians to officially *recognize* the region so as to strengthen Frankfurt's position in the global interurban competition. This call also provides a rationale for coherence and the idea of common interests among the many objectively disparate interests in the region: it displaces the conflicts among unequally advantaged sectors onto a project of regional competition with other regions. Regionalism then emerges as the concept for bridging the global orientation of leading sectors with the various local agendas of various constituencies in the region.

In contrast, the city discourse rather than the ideology of regionalism dominates in cities such as New York or Sao Paulo (see Toulouse, 1992). The challenge is how to bridge the inner city, or the squatters at the urban perimeter, with the center. In multiracial cities, multiculturalism has emerged as one form of this bridging. A "regional" discourse is perhaps beginning to emerge, but it has until now been totally submerged under the suburbanization banner, a concept that suggests both escape from and dependence on the city. The notion of conflict within the urban periphery among diverse interests and constituencies has not really been much of a factor in the United States. The delicate point at the level of the region has rather been the articulation between the residential suburbs and the city.

Contested Space

Large cities have emerged as strategic territories for these developments. *First, cities are the sites for concrete operations of the economy.* For our purposes we can distinguish two forms of such concrete operations: (1) In terms of economic globalization and place, cities are strategic places that concentrate command functions, global markets, and, as demonstrated in Chapter 4, production sites for the advanced corporate service industries. (2) In terms of day-to-day work in the leading industrial complex, finance, and specialized services, we saw in Chapter 6 that a large share of the jobs involved are low paid and manual, and many are held by women and immigrants. Although these types of workers and jobs are never represented as part of the global economy, they are in fact as much a part of globalization as international finance is. We see at work here a dynamic of valorization that has sharply increased the distance between the devalorized and the valorized—indeed overvalorized—sectors of the economy. These joint presences have made cities a contested terrain.

The structure of economic activity has brought about changes in the organization of work that are reflected in a pronounced shift in the job supply, with strong polarization occurring in the income distribution and occupational distribution of workers. Major growth industries show a greater incidence of jobs at the high- and low-paying ends of the scale than do the older industries now in decline. Almost half the jobs in the producer services are lower-income jobs, and the other half are in the two highest earnings classes. On the other hand, a large share of manufacturing workers were in middle-earning jobs during the postwar period of high growth in these industries in the United States and the United Kingdom.

One particular concern here was to understand how new forms of inequality actually are constituted into new social forms, such as gentrified neighborhoods, informal economies, or downgraded manufacturing sectors. To what extent these developments are connected to the consolidation of an economic complex oriented to the global market is difficult to say. Precise empirical documentation of the linkages or impacts is impossible; the effort here is focused, then, on a more general attempt to understand the consequences of both the ascendance of such an international economic complex and the general move to a service economy.

Second, the city concentrates diversity. Its spaces are inscribed with the dominant corporate culture but also with a multiplicity of other cultures and identities, notably through immigration. The slippage is evident: the dominant culture can encompass only part of the city. And while corporate power inscribes noncorporate cultures and identities with "otherness," thereby devaluing them, they are present everywhere. The immigrant communities and informal economy described in Chapter 6 are only two instances. Diverse cultures and ethnicities are especially strong in major cities in the United States and Western Europe; these also have the largest concentrations of corporate power.

We see here an interesting correspondence between great concentrations of corporate power and large concentrations of "others." It invites us to see that globalization is not only constituted in terms of capital and the new international corporate culture (international finance, telecommunications, information flows) but also in terms of people and noncorporate cultures. There is a whole infrastructure of low-wage, nonprofessional jobs and activities that constitutes a crucial part of the so-called corporate economy.

A focus on the *work* behind command functions, on *production* in the finance and services complex, and on market*places* has the effect of incorporating the material facilities underlying globalization and the whole infrastructure of jobs and workers typically not seen as belonging to the corporate sector of the economy: secretaries and cleaners, the truckers who deliver the software, the variety of technicians and repair workers, and all the jobs having to do with the maintenance, painting, and renovation of the buildings where it is all housed.

This expanded focus can lead to the recognition that a multiplicity of economies is involved in constituting the so-called global information economy. It recognizes types of activities, workers, and firms that have never been installed in the "center" of the economy or that have been evicted from that center in the restructuring of the 1980s and have therefore been devalued in a system that puts too much weight on a narrow conception of the center of the economy. Globalization can, then, be seen as a process that involves multiple economies and work cultures.

The preceding chapters have tried to demonstrate that cities are of great importance to the dominant economic sectors. Large cities in the highly developed world are the places where globalization processes assume concrete, localized forms. These localized forms are, in good part, what globalization is about. We can then think of cities also as the place where the contradictions of the internationalization of capital either come to rest or conflict. If we consider, further, that large cities also concentrate a growing share of disadvantaged populations—immigrants in both Europe and the United States; African Americans and Latinos in the United States—then we can see that cities have become a strategic terrain for a whole series of conflicts and contradictions.

On one hand, they concentrate a disproportionate share of corporate power and are one of the key sites for the overvalorization of the corporate economy; on the other, they concentrate a disproportionate share of the disadvantaged and are one of the key sites for their devalorization.

This joint presence happens in a context where (1) the internationalization of the economy has grown sharply and cities have become increasingly strategic for global capital; and (2) marginalized people have come into representation and are making claims on the city as well. This joint presence is further brought into focus by the sharpening of the distance between the two. The center now concentrates immense power, a power that rests on the capability for global control and the capability to produce superprofits. And marginality, notwithstanding weak economic and political power, has become an increasingly strong presence through the new politics of culture and identity.

If cities were irrelevant to the globalization of economic activity, the center could simply abandon them and not be bothered by all of this. Indeed, this is precisely what some politicians argue—that cities have become hopeless reservoirs for all kinds of social despair. It is interesting to note again how the dominant economic narrative argues that place no longer matters, that firms can be located anywhere thanks to telematics, that major industries now are information-based and hence not place-bound. This line of argument devalues cities at a time when they are major sites for the new cultural politics. It also allows the corporate economy to extract major concessions from city governments under the notion that firms can simply leave and relocate elsewhere, which is not quite the case for a whole complex of firms, as much of this book sought to show.

In seeking to show that (1) cities are strategic to economic globalization because they are command points, global marketplaces, and production sites for the information economy; and (2) many of the devalued sectors of the urban economy actually fulfill crucial functions for the center, this book attempts to recover the importance of cities specifically in a globalized economic system and the importance of those overlooked sectors that rest largely on the labor of women, immigrants, and, in the case of large U.S. cities, African Americans and Latinos. In fact it is the intermediary sectors of the economy (such as routine office work, headquarters that are not geared to the world markets, the variety of services demanded by the largely suburbanized middle class) and of the urban population (the middle class) that can and have left cities. The two sectors that have stayed, the center and the "other," find in the city the strategic terrain for their operations.

The tables that follow present data on a number of variables for select cities. The variables range from population size and numbers of foreign residents to basic quality-of-life indicators. The purpose is to provide additional information to that discussed in the main text of the book and, particularly, on aspects discussed only briefly in the text that may be of interest. Some of these variables may become of interest in the near future in a way they are not necessarily today; others provide what is conventionally considered important information, such as unemployment rates.

TABLE A.1

Resident and Nonresident Populations of Select Major Cities

City	Population (1980s)	Foreign Residents	Tourists (annual totals)
Abidjan	2,500,000 (1990 est.) 1,724,170 (1985)	750,000 (32% of population)	183,675 (1986)
Bangkok	5,775,000 (1989)	589,099	4,809,508 (1989)
Beijing	10,819,407 (July 1, 1990)	15,000 (including students, 1989)	645,000 (1989)
Bucharest	2,045,534 2,325,037 (includes suburbs, 1987)	800 residents 3,068 foreign students (1989)	1,195,268 (registered in hotels)
Buenos Aires	2,902,000 city 8,852,000 suburbs (1990)	n/a	722,626 (1985)
Cairo	6,406,000 (Dec. 17, 1989)	161,357	1,969,000 (1989)
Delhi	6,220,406 (1981 census)	n/a	1,163,744 (excluding Pakistan and Bangladesh, 1987)
Istanbul	7,600,000 (1990)	n/a	711,258 (by air and sea, 1986)
Jakarta	8,682,100 (1989)	32,739 residents 17,983 nonpermanent residents (1988)	522,079 (1988)
Kuala Lumpur	1,127,000 (1990)	n/a	3,673,024 (1989)
Lima	6,414,500 (1990 projection)	4,000 (nonimmigrants)	355,895 (for Peru)

(continued on next page)

TABLE A.1 (CONTINUED)

Resident and Nonresident Populations of Select Major Cities

City	Population (1980s)	Foreign Residents	Tourists (annual totals)
London (greater)	6,735,000 (1988)	23,700 net international migration (1988) 10% ethnic population	10.6 million from overseas (1989) 7.8 million from U.K.
Madrid	3,108,463 (1989)	61,024 (1987)	3,590,400 (1988)
Mexico City	8,236,960 (1990)	n/a	813,000 (1987)
Montreal	1,015,000 (1986 census)	n/a	6,000,000 (1989)
Nairobi	827,775 (1989 census)	183,818 (without Kenyan nationality)	400,000 (average)
New York (metro area)	7,263,000 (1986)	n/a	25,320,000 (1989)
Paris	2,152,333 (1990)	361,572 (1982)	20,000,000
Rome	2,811,646 (1989)	110,359 173,229 in province of Rome (1989)	4,626,000 (1988)
Sao Paulo (metro area)	17,941,096 (1990 est.)	924,389	n/a
Seoul	10,576,794 (Nov. 1, 1989)	10,195 (1989)	2,664,281 (1989)
Stockholm	672,000 (1989 est.)	48,107 born abroad (1988)	3,800,000 (1988)
Tokyo	11,854,987 (Oct. 1990)	181,815 (June 1988) 14,438 students	1,498,691 (1989 est.)
Vienna	1,531,648 (1988)	209,815 (1989)	6,920,845 (overnight stays, 1989)

Source: Governor of Tokyo and Summit Conference of Major Cities of the World, March 1991. *Major Cities of the World* (Tokyo: Tokyo Metropolitan Government).

TABLE A.2

Consumer and Employment Data

City	Unemployment 1990	Per Capita Income ($US)	Caloric Intake (CAL per day)
Abidjan	35%	1,208	2,038
Bangkok	145,400 people (1988)	3,235 (1989)	2,500–2,800
Beijing	.5% (48-hour week)	337	n/a
Bucharest	n/a	1,793	2,462
Buenos Aires	8.8%–5.7% (1988)	7,851	2,450
Cairo	2.3%/7.5% (potentially unemployed)	n/a	2,381
Delhi	794,000 (1989, applications at employment exchanges)	391	1,900
Istanbul	n/a	n/a	2,500
Jakarta	121,325 (seeking employment, 1988)	816.7	1,709
Kuala Lumpur	n/a	n/a	n/a
Lima	7.9% (1989; only 18.3% adequately employed)	n/a	n/a
London	4.5%	16,839.9 (1987)	2,190
Madrid	10.3%	13,000	2,800
Mexico City	3.7% (1989)	n/a	n/a
Montreal (Quebec)	9.3% (1989)	14,823	2,163
Nairobi	19.9% total 27.3% of women need jobs	n/a	n/a
New York	5.8% (1989)	11,188	n/a

(continued on next page)

TABLE A.2 (CONTINUED)

Consumer and Employment Data

City	Unemployment 1990	Per Capita Income ($US)	Caloric Intake (CAL per day)
Paris	10.4%	23,597	2,053.8
Rome	7.3% (1989)	17,309	n/a
Sao Paulo	8.2%/8.7% city/metro region (ratio of unemployed to economically active)	3,860	n/a
Seoul	5.5% (1989) 8.6% (1985) (59-hour week)	n/a	n/a
Stockholm	.6% (1989)	17,085	n/a
Tokyo	n/a	27,211	1,999
Vienna	5.4% (1988)	24,231	2,500–3,600

Source: Governor of Tokyo and Summit Conference of Major Cities of the World, March 1991. *Major Cities of the World* (Tokyo: Tokyo Metropolitan Government).

TABLE A.3

Consumer Prices

City	Year	Consumer Price Index	City	Year	Consumer Price Index
Abidjan	1983	100	Istanbul	1978/79	100
	1984	104.3		1985	1,309.3
	1985	106.2		1986	1,765.1
	1986	113.2		1987	2,490.1
	1987	119.3		1988	4,347
				1989	7,405.1
Bangkok	1986	100			
	1980	76.5	Jakarta	1977/78	100
	1985	98.3		1985	233.16
	1987	102.6		1986	252.82
	1988	106.5		1987	276.46
	1989	113.2		1988	288.91
Beijing	1980	100	Lima	1980	100
	1985	111.2		1987	114.5
	1986	100		1988	1,722.3
	1987	101.9		1989	2,775.3
	1988	114.3			
	1989	111.1	Madrid	1983	100
				1985	119.9
Bucharest	1985	100		1986	129.9
	1986	100.7		1987	135.5
	1987	101.9		1988	143.1
	1988	104.5		1989	153.7
	1989	105.4			
			Mexico City	1980	100
Buenos Aires	1986	100		1985	1,027.2
	1987	213.4		1986	1,899.6
	1988	473.4		1987	4,360.8
	1989	6,012.1		1988	9,271.7
				1989	11,161
Cairo	1985	100			
	1986	122.6	Montreal	1981	100
	1987	146.7		1985	128.1
	1988	173.7		1986	134.3
	1989	205.6		1987	140.4
				1988	145.8
Delhi	1980	100		1989	152.3
	1985	196			
	1986	211			
	1987	232			

(continued on next page)

T A B L E A . 3 (CONTINUED)

Consumer Prices

City	Year	Consumer Price Index	City	Year	Consumer Price Index
Nairobi	1980	100	Sao Paulo	Mar 1986	100
	1985	187.3		Dec 1986	130.5
	1986	195.9		1987	609.8
	1987	212.7		1988	6,047.5
	1989	254.4		1989	104,976.1
New York	1982/84	100			
	1985	108.7	Seoul	1980	100
	1986	112.3		1985	141.2
	1987	118.0		1986	145.1
	1988	123.7		1987	149.9
	1989	130.6		1988	160.2
				1989	169.1
Paris	1980	100			
	1985	156.9	Stockholm	1980	100
	1986	160.7		1985	153.8
	1987	166.0		1986	160.3
	1988	170.4		1987	167.0
	1989	176.5		1988	176.7
Rome	1980	100	Tokyo	1985	100
	1985	190.6		1986	100.9
	1986	202.3		1987	101.3
	1987	216		1988	102.3
	1988	222.1		1989	105.1
	1989	236.8			
			Vienna	1986	100
				1987	101.4
				1988	103.4

Source: Governor of Tokyo and Summit Conference of Major Cities of the World, March 1991. *Major Cities of the World* (Tokyo: Tokyo Metropolitan Government).

TABLE A.4

Quality-of-Life Information, 1987–1991[a]

City	Number of Housing Units	Criminal Offenses per Year	Number of Day Nurseries	Number of Hospital Beds	Number of Doctors	Annual Traffic Deaths
Abidjan	n/a	49,000	n/a	2,091	n/a	1,019
Bangkok	1,084,583	23,021 (1988)	n/a	n/a	4,861 (1988)	917 (1988)
Beijing	3,225 (1989)	9,241 (1989)	4,846	56,000	41,916 (1989)	262
Bucharest	n/a	5,087 (Jan–June, 1990)	348	27,352	3,599	180 (Jan–June, 1990)
Buenos Aires	1,216,325	110,243 (1988)	n/a	24,807 (1988)	n/a	3,750 (1988)
Cairo	1,734,100	n/a	184	24,901	3,132	n/a
Delhi	n/a	n/a	50 (1984–85)	19,000	n/a	1,581
Istanbul	n/a	n/a	n/a	24,173	13,534	n/a
Jakarta	1,783,194	35,270 (1988)	1,785 (1988–89)	15,377 (1988–89)	n/a	451 (1987)
Kuala Lumpur	n/a	7,000	273	4,226	3,608	62
Lima	872,550	86,530	n/a	14,873	13,114	832
London	2,782,000 (1986)	620,000 (1988)	9,100	n/a	7,553	742

(continued on next page)

TABLE A.4 (CONTINUED)

Quality-of-Life Information, 1987–1991[a]

City	Number of Housing Units	Criminal Offenses per Year	Number of Day Nurseries	Number of Hospital Beds	Number of Doctors	Annual Traffic Deaths
Madrid	308,733	99,394	4,619	13,937	19,984	454
Mexico City	2,017,972	71,598	191 (public)	21,551	22,488	n/a
Montreal	443,560	209,193	358	39,421	6,136	67
Nairobi	n/a	n/a	23	5,696	n/a	n/a
New York	2,992,169 (1992)	626,182 (1992)	3,000	34,863	24,279	566 (1992)
Paris	1,094,000	298,287 (1990)	465	88,972	35,352	104
Rome	1,015,769	379,320	137	38,773	n/a	n/a
Sao Paulo	1,312,107	n/a	564	239,504	18,544	8,863
Seoul	1,506,167	324,529	1,857	26,697	15,618	1,365
Stockholm	382,000	n/a	1,610	21,580	4,200	24
Tokyo	4,818,000	221,431	1,603	136,759	26,670	488
Vienna	n/a	34,460	14,996	21,720	8,221	81

[a]Figures are for 1991 unless otherwise specified.

Source: Governor of Tokyo and Summit Conference of Major Cities of the World, March 1991. *Major Cities of the World* (Tokyo: Tokyo Metropolitan Government).

TABLE A.5

The World's Largest Cities

City	Population (in thousands)	City	Population (in thousands)
Addis Ababa	1,912.5	Ho Chi Minh	2,700.9
Alexandria	3,295.0	Houston	1,630.5
Ankara	2,541.9		(3,711.0)
Atlanta	2,833.5	Hyderlead	(4,280.3)
Baghdad	1,984.1	Istanbul	6,293.4
Baltimore	2,382.1	Izmir	2,319.2
Bangalore	(4,086.6)	Karachi	(5,180.6)
Bangkok	5,876.0	Kiev	2,616.0
Beijing	5,531.5	Kinshasa	2,664
Belo Horizonte	2,415.9	La Habana (Cuba)	2,096
Berlin	3,433.7	Lima	(6,414.5)
Bombay	(12,571.7)	Liupanshui	2,107.1
Boston	4,171.6	London	6,794.4
	(574.3)	Los Angeles	3,485.4
Brasilia	1,803.8		(14,531.5)
Bucharest	2,127.2	Madrid	2,991.2
Budapest	2,017.4	Madurai	(5,361.5)
Buenos Aires	2,901.2	Manila	1,876.2
Cairo	6,663.0	Melbourne	3,080.1
Calcutta	(10,916.3)	Mexico City	(13,878.9)
Capetown	1,911.5	Miami	358
Caracas	1,824.8		(3,192.5)
	(2,784.0)	Minneapolis	370
Casablanca	2,263		(2,464.1)
Chengdu	2,499.0	Monterrey	(2,001.5)
Chicago	2,783.7	Montreal	(3,021.3)
	(8,065.6)	Moscow	8,801.0
Chongging	2,673.1	Nagasaki	2,154.8
Cleveland	505.6	Nanjiang	2,091.4
	(2,759.8)	New York City	7,322.6
Dallas	1,006.8		(18,087.2)
	(3,885.4)	Osaka	2,623.8
Delhi	(8,375.2)	Paris	2,189.0
Detroit	1,027.9	Philadelphia	1,585.6
	(4,665.2)		(5,899.3)
Fortaleza	1,825.0	Phoenix	983.4
Giza	2,096.0		(2,122.1)
Guadalajara	(2,264.6)	Pittsburgh	369.9
Guangzhou	3,181.5		(2,242.8)
Harbin	2,519.1	Pusan	3,514.8

(continued on next page)

T A B L E A . 5 (CONTINUED)

The World's Largest Cities

City	Population (in thousands)	City	Population (in thousands)
Rio de Janeiro	6,042.4	Suncheon	9,639.1
Roma	2,828.7	Surabaja	2,027.9
Salvador (Brazil)	2,050.1	Sydney	3,656.5
San Diego	1,110.5	Taego	2,029.8
	(2,498.0)	Tashkent	2,094.0
Santa Fe de Bogota	(4,176.8)	Teheran	6,042.6
Santiago	4,385.5	Tianjin	5,152.2
Sao Paolo	11,128.9	Tokyo	8,278.1
Shanghai	6,293.0	Toronto	(3,666.6)
Shenyang	3,944.2	Wuhan	3,287.7
Singapore	2,763.0	Xi'an	2,185.0
St. Louis	397	Yangon	2,513.0
	(2,444.1)	Yokohoma	3,220.3
St. Petersburg	4,468.0	Zibo	2,197.7

Note: Figures in parentheses indicate populations of the urban/suburban core (as compared to the metropolitan district).

Source: Demagraphic Yearbook (New York: Department of Economic and Social Affairs, Statistical Office, United Nations, 1991).

Select Cities of the World

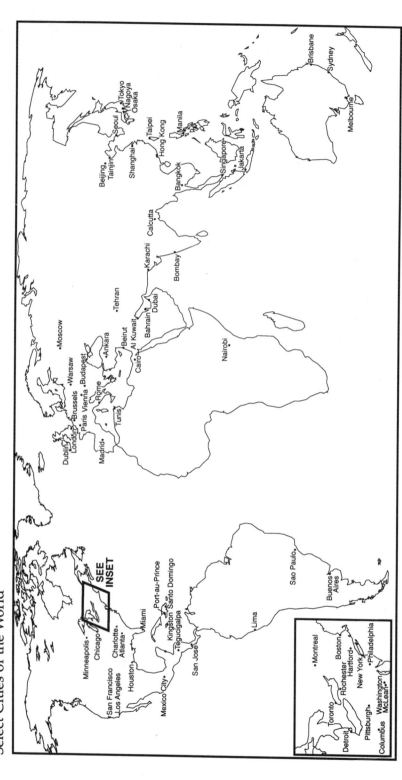

References

Abreu, A., M. Cocco, C. Despradel, E. G. Michael, and A. Peguero (1989). *Las Zonas Francas Industriales: El Exito de una Politica Economica.* Santo Domingo: Centro de Orientacion Economica.

Abu-Lughod, J. L. (1980). *Rabat: Urban Apartheid in Morocco.* Princeton: Princeton University Press.

Adrian, C. (1984). *Urban Impacts of Foreign and Local Investment in Australia* (Publication 119). Canberra: Australian Institute of Urban Studies.

Amin, Ash, and Kevin Robins. (1990). "The Re-Emergence of Regional Economies? The Mythical Geography of Flexible Accumulation." *Environment and Planning D: Society and Space, 8,* 1 (March), 7–34.

AMPO. (1988). "Japan's Human Imports: As Capital Flows Out, Foreign Labor Flows In." Special issue of *Japan-Asia Quarterly Review, 19* (1).

Asian Women's Association. (1988). "Women from Across the Seas: Migrant Workers in Japan." Tokyo: Asian Women's Association.

Bagnasco, Arnaldo. (1977). *Tre Italie: La Problematica Territoriale Dello Sviluppo Italiano.* Bologna: Il Mulino.

Bailey, Thomas. (1990). "Jobs of the Future and the Education They Will Require: Evidence from Occupational Forecasts." *Educational Researcher, 20* (2), 11–20.

Balbo, Laura, and Luigi Manconi. (1990). *I Razzismi Possibili.* Milano: Feltrinelli.

Bank for International Settlements. (1992). *62nd Annual Report.* Basel: B. I. S.

Bavishi, V., and H. E. Wyman. (1983). *Who Audits the World: Trends in the Worldwide Accounting Profession.* Storrs, CT: University of Connecticut, Center for Transnational Accounting and Financial Research.

Beneria, Lourdes. (1989). "Subcontracting and Employment Dynamics in Mexico City." In A. Portes et al. (Eds.), *The Informal Economy: Studies in Advanced and Less Developed Countries.* Baltimore: Johns Hopkins University Press.

Benko, Georges, and Mick Dunford (Eds.). (1991). *Industrial Change and Regional Development: The Transformation of New Industrial Spaces.* London and New York: Belhaven Press/Pinter.

Berger, Suzanne and Michael J. Piore. (1980). *Dualism and Discontinuity in Industrial Societies.* New York and London: Cambridge University Press.

Berque, Augustin. (1987). *La Qualite de la Ville: Urbanite Francaise, Urbanite Nippone.* Tokyo: Maison Franco-Japonaise.

Bestor, Theodore. (1989). *Neighborhood Tokyo*. Stanford, CA: Stanford University Press.

Bhagwati, J. (1988). *Protectionism*. Boston: MIT Press.

Blaschke, J., and A. Germershausen. (1989). "Migration und ethnische Beziehungen." *Nord-Sud Aktuell*, 3–4.

Blumberg, P. (1981). *Inequality in an Age of Decline*. New York: Oxford University Press.

Body-Gendrot, S. (1993). *Ville et Violence*. Paris: Presses Universitaires de France.

Body-Gendrot, Sophie, Emmanuel Ma Mung, and Catherine Hodier (Eds.). (1992). "Entrepreneurs Entre Deux Mondes: Les Creations d'Entreprises par les Etrangers: France, Europe, Amerique du Nord." Special Issue, *Revue Europeenne des Migrations Internationales, 8* (1), 5–8.

Boissevain, Jeremy. (1992). "Les Entreprises Ethniques aux Pays-Bas." *Revue Europeenne des Migrations Internationales, 8* (1), 97–106.

Bourgeois, P. (Forthcoming). *In Search of Respect: Selling Crack in El Barrio*. Structural Analysis in the Social Sciences Series. New York: Cambridge University Press.

Boyer, Christine. (1983). *Dreaming the Rational City*. Cambridge, MA: MIT Press.

Boyer, Robert (Ed.). (1986). *La Flexibilite du Travail en Europe*. Paris: La Decouverte.

Brosnan, P., and F. Wilkinson. (1987). *Cheap Labour: Britain's False Economy*. London: Low Pay Unit.

Brown, C. (1984). *Black and White Britain*. London: Heinemann.

Brusco, Sabastiano. (1986). "Small Firms and Industrial Districts: The Experience of Italy." In David Keeble and Francis Weever (Eds.), *New Firms and Regional Development*. London: Croom Helm.

Buck, Nick, Matthew Drennan, and Kenneth Newton. (1992). "Dynamics of the Metropolitan Economy." In Susan Fainstein, Ian Gordon, and Michael Harloe (Eds.) *Divided Cities: New York & London in the Contemporary World*. Oxford: Blackwell.

Burgel, Guy. (1993). *La Ville Aujourd'hui*. Paris: Hachette, Collection Pluriel.

Canadian Urban Institute. (1993). *Disentangling Local Government Responsibilities: International Comparisons*. Toronto: Canadian Urban Institute, Urban Focus Series 93-1.

Canevari, Annapaola. (1991). "Immigrati Prima Accoglienza: E Dopo?" *Dis T Rassegna di Studi e Ricerche del Dipartimento di Scienze del Territorio del Politecnico di Milano, 9* (Settembre), 53–60.

Cardew, R. V., J. V. Langdale, and D. C. Rich (Eds.). (1982). *Why Cities Change: Urban Development and Economic Change in Sydney*. Sydney: Allen & Unwin.

Carleial, L., and M. R. Nabuco (Orgs.). (1989). *Transformacoes na Divisao Inter-regional no Brasil*. Sao Paulo: Anpec/Caen/Cedeplar.

Castells, M. (1983). *The City and the Grassroots: A Cross-Cultural Theory of Urban Social Movements*. Berkeley: University of California Press.

Castells, M. (1989). *The Informational City*. London: Blackwell.

CEMAT. (1988). *Draft European Regional Planning Strategy*. Vols. 1 and 2. Luxembourg: CEMAT.

Chase-Dunn, C. (1984). "Urbanization in the World System: New Directions for Research." In M. P. Smith (Ed.), *Cities in Transformation*. Newbury Park, CA: Sage.

Cheshire, P. C., and D. G. Hay. (1989). *Urban Problems in Western Europe*. London: Unwin Hyman.

City of Toronto. (1990). *Cityplan '91: Central Area Trends Report*. Toronto: City of Toronto, Planning and Development Department (February).

Clavel, P. (1986). *The Progressive City*. New Brunswick, NJ: Rutgers University Press.

Cobos, Emilio Pradilla. (1984). *Contribucion a la Critica de la "Teoria Urbana": Del "Espacio" a la "Crisis Urbana."* Mexico, D.F.: Universidad Autonoma Metropolitana Xochimilco.

Cohen, R. (1987). *The New Helots: Migrants in the International Division of Labour*. London: Avebury.

Cohen, Stephen S., and John Zysman. (1987). *Manufacturing Matters: The Myth of the Post-Industrial Economy*. New York: Basic Books.

Colomina, Beatriz (Ed.). (1992). *Sexuality & Space*. Princeton Papers on Architecture. Princeton, NJ: Princeton Architectural Press.

Colon, Alice, Marya Munoz, Neftali Garcia, and Idsa Alegria. (1988). "Trayectoria de la Participacion Laboral de las Mujeres en Puerto Rico de los Anos 1950 a 1985." In *Crisis, Sociedad y Mujer: Estudio Comparativo entre Paises de America (1950–1985)*. Havana: Federacion de Mujeres Cubanas.

Corbridge, S., and J. Agnew. (1991). "The U. S. Trade and Budget Deficit in Global Perspective: An Essay in Geopolitical Economy." *Environment and Planning D: Society and Space, 9*, 71–90.

Cornelius, Wayne, et al. (1992). "Controlling Illegal Immigration: A Global Perspective." Work in Progress, Center for United States–Mexican Studies, University of California, San Diego.

Daly, M. T., and R. Stimson. (1992). "Sydney: Australia's Gateway and Financial Capital." In E. Blakely and T. J. Stimpson (Eds.), *New Cities of the Pacific Rim* (Chap. 18). Berkeley: University of California, Institute for Urban & Regional Development.

Daniels, Peter W. (1985). *Service Industries: A Geographical Appraisal*. London and New York: Methuen.

Daniels, Peter W. (1991). "Producer Services and the Development of the Space Economy." In Peter W. Daniels and Frank Moulaert (Eds.), *The Changing Geography of Advanced Producer Services*. London and New York: Belhaven Press.

Dauhajre, Andres, E. Riley, R. Mena, and J. A. Guerrero. (1989). *Impacto Economico de las Zonas Francas Industriales de Exportacion en la Republica Dominicana*. Santo Domingo: Fundacion Economia y Desarrollo, Inc.

Deecke, H., T. Kruger, and D. Lapple. (1993). "Alternative Szenarien der wirtschaftlichen Strukturentwicklung in der Hamburger Wirtschaft unter raumlichen Gesichtspunkten." Final Report for the City of Hamburg. Hamburg: Technische Universitat HamburgHarburg (July).

Deere, Carmen Diana, Peggy Antrobus, Lynn Bolles, Edwin Melendez, Peter Phillips, Marcia Rivera, and Helen Safa. (1990). *In the Shadows of the Sun: Caribbean Development Alternatives and U.S. Policy.* Boulder, CO: Westview.

Delauney, Jean Claude, and Jean Gadrey. (1987). *Les Enjeux de la Societe de Service.* Paris: Presses de la Fondation des Sciences Politiques.

Dogan, M., and J. D. Kasarda (Eds.). (1988). *A World of Giant Cities.* Newbury Park, CA: Sage.

Dore, Ronald. (1986). *Flexible Rigidities: Industrial Policy and Structural Adjustment in the Japanese Economy, 1970–1980.* London: Athlone Press.

Drache, D., and M. Gertler (Eds.). (1991). *The New Era of Global Competition: State Policy and Market Power.* Montreal: McGill-Queen's University Press.

Drennan, Mathew P. (1989). "Information Intensive Industries in Metropolitan Areas of the United States." *Environment and Planning A, 21,* 1603–1618.

Drennan, Mathew P. (1992). "Gateway Cities: The Metropolitan Sources of U.S. Producer Service Exports." *Urban Studies, 29* (2), 217–235.

Duarte, R. (1989). "Heterogeneidade no Setor Informal: Um Estudo de Micro-unidades Produtivas em Aracaju e Teresina." *Estudios Economicos,* Fipe, No. 19, Numero Especial, pp. 99–123.

duRivage, Virginia L. (Ed.). (1992). *New Policies for the Part-Time and Contingent Workforce.* Washington, DC: Economic Policy Institute.

Edel, Matthew. (1986). "Capitalism, Accumulation and the Explanation of Urban Phenomena." In Michael Dear and Allen Scott (Eds.), *Urbanization and Urban Planning in Capitalist Society.* New York: Methuen.

El-Shakhs, Salah. (1972). "Development, Primacy and Systems of Cities." *Journal of Developing Areas, 7* (October), 11–36.

Eurocities. (1989). *Documents and Subjects of Eurocities Conference.* Barcelona, April 21–22.

European Institute of Urban Affairs. (1992). *Urbanisation and the Functions of Cities in the European Community: A Report to the Commission of the European Communities, Directorate General for Regional Policy (XVI).* Liverpool: Liverpool John Moores University, April.

Fainstein, S. (1993). *The City Builders.* Oxford: Blackwell.

Fainstein, S., N. Fainstein, R. C. Hill, D. R. Judd, and M. P. Smith. (1986). *Restructuring the City* (2nd ed.). New York: Longman.

Fainstein, S., I. Gordon, and M. Harloe. (1992). *Divided Cities: Economic Restructuring and Social Change in London and New York.* New York: Blackwell.

Fernandez-Kelly, M. P., and A. M. Garcia. (1989). "Informalization at the Core: Hispanic Women, Homework, and the Advanced Capitalist State." In A. Portes et al. (Eds.), *The Informal Economy: Studies in Advanced and Less Developed Countries.* Baltimore: Johns Hopkins University Press.

Fernandez-Kelly, M. P., and Saskia Sassen. (1992). "Immigrant Women in the Garment and Electronic Industries in the New York–New Jersey Region and in Southern California." Final Research Report presented to the Ford, Revson, and Tinker Foundations. New York, June.

Friedmann, John. (1986). "The World City Hypothesis." *Development and Change, 17,* 69–84.

Friedmann, J., and G. Wolff. (1982). "World City Formation: An Agenda for Research and Action." *International Journal of Urban and Regional Research, 15* (1), 269–283.

Frost, Martin, and Nigel Spence. (1992). "Global City Characteristics and Central London's Employment." *Urban Studies, 30* (3), 547–558.

Fujita, Kuniko. (1991). "A World City and Flexible Specialization: Restructuring of the Tokyo Metropolis." *International Journal of Urban and Regional Research 15* (1), 269–284.

Gad, Gunter. (1991). "Toronto's Financial District." *Canadian Urban Landscapes, 1,* 203–207.

Gans, Herbert. (1984). "American Urban Theory and Urban Areas." In Ivan Szelenyi (Ed.), *Cities in Recession.* Newbury Park, CA: Sage.

Garofalo, G., and M. S. Fogarty. (1979). "Urban Income Distribution and the Urban Hierarchy-Inequality Hypothesis." *Review of Economics and Statistics, 61,* 381–388.

Gerlach, Michael. (1992). *Alliance Capitalism: The Social Organization of Japanese Business.* Berkeley: University of California Press.

Gershuny, Jonathan, and Ian Miles. (1983). *The New Service Economy: The Transformation of Employment in Industrial Societies.* New York: Praeger.

Giarini, Orio (Ed.). (1987). *The Emerging Service Economy.* Oxford and New York: Pergamon Press.

Giddens, A. (1991). *The Consequences of Modernity.* Oxford: Polity Press.

Gillette, A., and A. Sayad. (1984). *L'Immigration Algerienne en France* (2nd ed.). Paris: Editions Entente.

Glickman, N. J. (1979). *The Growth and Management of the Japanese Urban System.* New York: Academic Press.

Glickman, N. J., and A. K. Glasmeier. (1989). "The International Economy and the American South." In L. Rodwin and H. Sazanami (Eds.), *Deindustrialization and Regional Economic Transformation: The Experience of the United States.* Winchester, MA: Unwin Hyman.

Glickman, N. J., and D. P. Woodward. (1989). *The New Competitors: How Foreign Investors Are Changing the U.S. Economy.* New York: Basic Books.

Goddard, J. B. (1993). "Information and Communications Technologies, Corporate Hierarchies and Urban Hierarchies in the New Europe." Presented at the Fourth International Workshop on Technological Change and Urban Form: Productive and Sustainable Cities, Berkeley, CA, April 14–16.

Goldsmith, William V., and Edward J. Blakely. (1992). *Separate Societies: Poverty and Inequality in U. S. Cities.* Philadelphia: Temple University Press.

Goldthorpe, John (Ed.). (1984). *Order and Conflict in Contemporary Capitalism*. Oxford: Clarendon Press.

Gordon, Ian, and Saskia Sassen. (1992). "Restructuring the Urban Labor Markets." In S. Fainstein et al. (Eds.), *Divided Cities: New York and London in the Contemporary World* (pp. 105–128). Oxford: Blackwell.

Graham, Edward M., and Paul R. Krugman. (1989). *Foreign Direct Investment in the United States*. Washington, DC: Institute for International Economics.

Granovetter, Mark. (1985). "Economic Action and Social Structure: The Problem of Embeddedness." *American Journal of Sociology, 91*, 481–510.

Gregory, Derek, and John Urry (Eds.). (1985). *Social Relations and Spatial Structures*. London: Macmillan.

Grosfoguel, Ramon. (1993). "World Cities in the Caribbean City System: Miami and San Juan." Paper presented at the conference on World Cities in a World System, Blacksburg, VA, April.

Grosz, E. (1992). "Bodies-Cities." In Beatriz Colomina (Ed.), *Sexuality & Space* (pp. 241–253). Princeton Papers on Architecture. Princeton, NJ: Princeton Architectural Press.

Hall, Peter. (1964). *Greater London*. London: Faber and Faber.

Hall, Peter. (1966). *The World Cities*. New York: McGraw-Hill.

Hall, Peter. (1988). *Cities of Tomorrow*. Oxford: Blackwell.

Hall, P., and D. Hay. (1980). *Growth Centers in the European Urban System*. London: Heinemann Educational Books.

Hall, S. (1991). "The Local and the Global: Globalization and Ethnicity." In Anthony D. King (Ed.), *Current Debates in Art History 3. Culture, Globalization and the World-System: Contemporary Conditions for the Representation of Identity*. Department of Art and Art History, State University of New York at Binghamton.

Hardoy, J. E. (1975). *Urbanization in Latin America*. Garden City, NJ: Anchor Books.

Hardoy, J. E., and D. Satterthwaite. (1989). *Squatter Citizen: Life in the Urban Third World*. London: Earthscan Publications.

Harris, R. (1991). "The Geography of Employment and Residence in New York Since 1950." In J. Mollenkopf and M. Castells (Eds.), *Dual City: Restructuring New York* (pp. 129–152). New York: Russell Sage Foundation.

Harrison, B., and B. Bluestone. (1988). *The Great U-Turn*. New York: Basic Books.

Hartmann, Heidi (Ed.). (1987). *Computer Chips and Paper Clips: Technology and Women's Employment*. Washington, DC: National Academy Press.

Harvey, David. (1985). *The Urbanization of Capital*. Oxford: Blackwell.

Harvey, David. (1989). *The Condition of Postmodernity*. Oxford: Blackwell.

Hausserman, Hartmut, and Walter Siebel. (1987). *Neue Urbanitat*. Frankfurt: Suhrkamp Verlag.

Henderson, Jeff, and Manuel Castells (Eds.). (1987). *Global Restructuring and Territorial Development*. London: Sage.

Hill, R.C. (1989). "Comparing Transnational Production Systems: The Case of the Automobile Industry in the United States and Japan." *International Journal of Urban and Regional Research, 13* (3), 462.

Hino, Masateru. (1984). "The Location of Head and Branch Offices of Large Enterprises in Japan." *Science Reports of Tohoku University (Senday, Japan). Geography Series, 34* (2).

Hirst, Paul, and Jonathan Zeitlin. (1989). *Reversing Industrial Decline?* Oxford: Berg.

Hollifield, James F. (1992). *Immigrants, Markets, and States: The Political Economy of Postwar Europe.* Cambridge, MA: Harvard University Press.

Hymer, Stephen, and Robert Rowthorn. (1970). "Multinational Corporations and International Oligopoly." In Charles P. Kindleberger (Ed.), *The International Corporation.* Cambridge, MA: MIT Press.

Ishizuka, H., and Y. Ishida. (1988). *Tokyo: Urban Growth and Planning, 1968–1988.* Tokyo: Center for Urban Studies, Tokyo Metropolitan University.

Ito, Tatsuo, and Masafumi Tanifuji. (1982). "The Role of Small and Intermediate Cities in National Development in Japan." In O. P. Mathur (Ed.), *Small Cities and National Development.* Nagoya: UNCRD.

Iyotani, Toshio. (1989). "The New Immigrant Workers in Tokyo." Typescript, Tokyo University of Foreign Studies.

Iyotani, Toshio, and Toshio Naito. (1989). "Tokyo no Kokusaika de Tenkan Semarareru Chusho Kigyo" [Medium- and small-sized corporations under pressure of change by Tokyo's internationalization]. *Ekonomisuto* (September 5), 44–49.

Japan Ministry of Labor. (1987). *Monthly Labor Statistics and Research Bulletin.* Tokyo: Ministry of Labor.

Jenkins, Rhys. (1991). "The Political Economy of Industrialization: A Comparison of Latin American and East Asian Newly Industrializing Countries." *Development and Change, 11,* 197–231.

Jonas, S. (1992). *The Battle for Guatemala: Rebels, Death Squads, and U.S. Power.* Boulder, CO: Westview Press.

Kasarda, John D., and Edward M. Crenshaw. (1991). "Third World Urbanization: Dimensions, Theories and Determinants." *Annual Review of Sociology, 17,* 467–501.

Keil, Roger, and Klaus Ronneberger. (1992). "Going Up the Country: Internationalization and Urbanization on Frankfurt's Northern Fringe." Presented at the UCLA International Sociological Association, Research Committee 29, *A New Urban and Regional Hierarchy? Impacts of Modernization, Restructuring and the End of Bipolarity,* April 24–26.

Keil, Roger, and Klaus Ronneberger. (1993). "The City Turned Inside Out: Spatial Strategies and Local Politics." In H. Hitz, R. Keil, V. Lehrer, K. Ronneberger, C. Schmid, and R. Wolff (Eds.), *Financial Metropoles in Restructuring: Zurich and Frankfurt en Route to Postfordism.* Zurich: Rotpunkt Publishers.

Kelly, Maryellen R. (1989). "Alternative Forms of Work Organization Under Programmable Automation." In Stephen Wood (Ed.), *The Transformation of Work?* (pp. 235–246). London: Unwin-Hyman.

Knight, R. V., and G. Gappert (Eds). (1989). *Cities in a Global Society.* Vol. 35. Urban Affairs Annual Reviews. Newbury Park, CA: Sage.

Komai, Hiroshi. (1992). "Are Foreign Trainees in Japan Disguised Cheap Laborers?" *Migration World, XX* (1), 13–17.

Komori, S. (1983). "Inner City in Japanese Context." *City Planning Review, 125,* 11–17.

Kowarick, L., A. M. Campos, and M. C. de Mello. (1991). "Os Percursos de Desigualdade." In R. Rolnik, L. Kowarick, and N. Somekh (Eds.), *Sao Paulo, Crise e Mudanca.* Sao Paulo: Brasiliense.

Kunzmann, K. R., and M. Wegener. (1991). "The Pattern of Urbanisation in Western Europe 1960–1990." Report for the Directorate General XVI of the Commission of the European Communities as part of the study *Urbanisation and the Function of Cities in the European Community.* Dortmund, Germany: Institut fur Raumplanung, March 15.

KUPI. (1981). *Policy for Revitalization of Inner City.* Kobe: Kobe Urban Problems Institute.

Kuttner, Robert. (1991). *The End of Laissez-Faire.* New York: Knopf.

Landell-Mills, Pierre, Ramgopal Agarwala, and Stanley Please. (1989). *Sub-Saharan Africa: From Crisis to Sustainable Growth.* Washington, DC: World Bank.

Lash, Scott, and John Urry. (1987). *The End of Organized Capitalism.* Cambridge: Polity Press.

Lavinas, Lena, and Maria Regina Nabuco. (1992). "Economic Crisis and Flexibility in Brazilian Labor Markets." Presented at the UCLA International Sociological Association, Research Committee 29, *A New Urban and Regional Hierarchy? Impacts of Modernization, Restructuring and the End of Bipolarity,* April 24–26.

Leborgne, D., and A. Lipietz. (1988). "L'Apres-Fordisme et son Espace." *Les Temps Modernes, 43,* 75–114.

Lee, Kyu Sik. (1989). *The Location of Jobs in a Developing Metropolis: Patterns of Growth in Bogota and Cali, Colombia.* New York: Oxford University Press.

Levy, Frank, and Richard Murname. (1992). "U.S. Earnings Levels and Earnings Inequality: A Review of Recent Trends and Proposed Explanations." *Journal of Economic Literature* (Sept.), 1333–1381.

Leyshon, A., P. Daniels, and N. Thrift. (1987). "Large Accountancy Firms in the U.K.: Spatial Development." Working Paper, St. David's University College, Lampeter, U.K., and University of Liverpool.

Lipietz, A. (1988). "New Tendencies in the International Division of Labor: Regimes of Accumulation and Modes of Regulation." In A. Scott and M. Storper (Eds.), *Production, Work, Territory.* Boston: Allen & Unwin.

Light, I., and E. Bonacich. (1988). *Immigrant Enterprise*. Berkeley: University of California Press.

Linn, Johannes F. (1983). *Cities in the Developing World: Policies for Their Equitable and Efficient Growth*. New York and Oxford: Oxford University Press.

Logan, J. R., and H. Molotch. (1987). *Urban Fortunes*. Berkeley: University of California Press.

Lomnitz, Larissa. (1985). "Mechanisms of Articulation between Shantytown Settlers and the Urban System." *Urban Anthropology, 7*, 185–205.

Lozano, Beverly. (1989). *The Invisible Work Force: Transforming American Business with Outside and Home-Based Workers*. New York: The Free Press.

Lozano, Wilfredo, and Isis Duarte. (1991). "Proceso de Urbanizacion, Modelos de Desarrollo y Clases Sociales en Republica Dominicana: 1960–1990." Paper presented at the seminar on Urbanization in the Caribbean in the Years of Crisis, Florida International University, Miami, May 29–June 1.

Machimura, Takashi. (1992). "The Urban Restructuring Process in the 1980s: Transforming Tokyo into a World City," *International Journal of Urban and Regional Research, 16* (1), 114–128.

Marcuse, Peter. (1986). "Abandonment, Gentrification, and Displacement: The Linkages in New York City." In Neil Smith and Peter Williams (Eds.), *Gentrification of the City*. Boston: Allen & Unwin.

Marie, Claude-Valentin. (1992). "Les Etrangers Non-Salaries en France, Symbole de la Mutation Economique des Annees 80." *Revue Europeenne des Migrations Internationales, 8* (1), 27–38.

Markusen, A. (1985). *Profit Cycles, Oligopoly, and Regional Development*. Cambridge, MA: MIT Press.

Markusen, A., and V. Gwiasda. (1993). "Multipolarity and the Layering of Functions in the World Cities: New York City's Struggle to Stay on Top." Presented in Tokyo at the Conference *New York, Tokyo and Paris*, October 1991.

Markusen, A., P. Hall, and A. Glasmeier. (1986). *High Tech America: The What, How, Where and Why of the Sunrise Industries*. London/Boston: Allen & Unwin.

Markusen, A., P. Hall, S. Campbell, and S. Deitrick (Eds.). (1991). *The Rise of the Gunbelt*. New York: Oxford University Press.

Marlin, John Tepper, Immanuel Ness, and Stephen T. Collins. (1986). *Book of World City Rankings*. New York: Macmillan.

Marshall, J. N., et al. (1986). *Uneven Development in the Service Economy: Understanding the Location and Role of Producer Services*. Report of the Producer Services Working Party, Institute of British Geographers and the ESRC, August.

Martinelli, Flavia, and Erica Schoenberger. (1991). "Oligopoly Is Alive and Well: Notes for a Broader Discussion of Flexible Accumulation." In Georges Benko and Mick Dunford (Eds.), *Industrial Change and Regional Development: The Transformation of New Industrial Spaces* (Chap. 6). London and New York: Belhaven Press/Pinter.

Masser, I., O. Sviden, and M. Wegener. (1990). *Europe 2020: Long-Term Scenarios of Transport and Communications in Europe.* Unpublished paper for the European Science Foundation.

Massey, Doreen. (1984). *Spatial Divisions of Labour: Social Structures and the Geography of Production.* London: Macmillan.

Mayer, Margit. (Forthcoming). "Shifts in the Local Political System in European Cities Since the 80s." In Mick Dunford and Grigoris Kafkalas (Eds.), *Competition, Regulation and the New Europe.* London: Belhaven.

Melendez, E., C. Rodriguez, and J. B. Figueroa. (1991). *Hispanics in the Labor Force.* New York: Plenum Press.

Meyer, David R. (1991). "Change in the World System of Metropolises: The Role of Business Intermediaries." *Urban Geography, 12* (5), 393–416.

Meyer, John R., and James M. Gustafson (Eds). (1988). *The U.S. Business Corporation: An Institution in Transition.* Cambridge, MA: Ballinger.

Mingione, E. (1991). *Fragmented Societies: A Sociology of Economic Life beyond the Market Paradigm.* Oxford: Blackwell.

Mingione, E., and E. Pugliese. (1988). "La Questione Urbana e Rurale: Tra Superamento Teorico e Problemi di Confini Incerti." *La Critica Sociologica, 85,* 17–50.

Mioni, Alberto. (1991). "Legittimita ed Efficacia del Progetto Urbano." *Dis T Rassegna di Studi e Ricerche del Dipartimento di Scienze del Territorio del Politecnico di Milano, 9* (Settembre), 137–150.

Mitter, S. (Ed.). (1989). *Information Technology and Women's Employment: The Case of the European Clothing Industry.* Berlin and New York: Springer Verlag.

Miyajima, Takashi. (1989). *The Logic of Receiving Foreign Workers: Among Dilemmas of Advanced Societies* (Gaikokujin Rodosha Mukaeire no Ronri: Senshin shakai no Jirenma no naka de). Tokyo: Akashi Shoten.

Montgomery, Cynthia A., and Michael E. Porter (Eds.). (1991). *Strategy: Seeking and Securing Competitive Advantage.* Boston: Harvard Business School Press.

Morita, Kiriro. (1992). "Japan and the Problem of Foreign Workers." Research Institute for the Japanese Economy, Faculty of Economics, University of Tokyo-Hongo.

Morita, Kiriro. (1993). "Foreign Workers in Japan." In S. Sassen (Ed.), *Labor Migration and Capital Mobility: Comparing the U.S. and Japan.* Special Issue of the *International Journal of Political Economy.*

Morita, Kiriro, and Saskia Sassen. (1994). "The New Illegal Immigration in Japan: A Research Report." *International Migration Review* (Forthcoming).

Morris, M. (1992). "Great Moments in Social Climbing: King Kong and the Human Fly." In Beatriz Colomina (Ed.), *Sexuality and Space.* Princeton Papers on Architecture. Princeton, NJ: Princeton Architectural Press.

Mowery, David (Ed.). (1988). *International Collaborative Ventures in U.S. Manufacturing.* Cambridge, MA: Ballinger.

Nabuco, M. R., A. F. Machado, and J. Pires. (1991). "Estrategias de Vida e Sobrevivencia na Industria de Confeccoes de Belo Horizonte." Belo Horizonte, Brazil: Cedeplar/UFMG.

Nakabayashi, Itsuki. (1987). "Social-Economic and Living Conditions of Tokyo's Inner City." *Geographical Reports of Tokyo Metropolitan University*, no. 22.

Nanami, Tadashi, and Yasuo Kuwabara (Eds.). (1989). *Tomorrow's Neighbors: Foreign Workers* (Asu no Rinjin: Gaikokujin Rodosha). Tokyo: Toyo Keizai Shimposha.

Nelson, J. I., and J. Lorence. (1985). "Employment in Service Activities and Inequality in Metropolitan Areas." *Urban Affairs Quarterly, 21,* (1), 106–125.

Noyelle, T., and A. B. Dutka. (1988). *International Trade in Business Services: Accounting, Advertising, Law and Management Consulting.* Cambridge, MA: Ballinger.

O'Connor, K. (1990). *State of Australia.* Clayton: National Centre for Australian Studies, Monash University.

Oliver, Nick, and Barry Wilkinson. (1988). *The Japanization of British Industry.* Oxford: Blackwell.

Parkinson, M., B. Foley, and D. R. Judd (Eds.). (1989). *Regenerating the Cities: The U.K. Crisis and the U.S. Experience.* Glenview, IL: Scott Foresman.

Perez-Sainz, J. P. (1992). *Informalidad Urbana en America Latina: Enfoques, Problematicas e Interrogantes.* Caracas: Editorial Nueva Sociedad.

Perez-Stable, Marifeli, and Miren Uriarte. (1993). "Cubans and the Changing Economy of Miami." In Rebecca Morales and Frank Bonilla (Eds.), *Latinos in a Changing U.S. Economy: Comparative Perspectives on Growing Inequality* (pp. 133–159). Sage Series on Race and Ethnic Relations, Vol. 7. Newbury Park, CA: Sage.

Petrella, R. (1990). "Technology and the Firm." *Technology Analysis & Strategic Management, 2,* 2.

Pickvance, C., and E. Preteceille (Eds). (1991). *State Restructuring and Local Power: A Comparative Perspective.* London: Pinter.

Polanyi, Karl. (1975). *The Great Transformation: The Political and Economic Origins of Our Time.* Boston: Beacon Press.

Portes, A., M. Castells, and L. Benton (Eds.). (1989). *The Informal Economy: Studies in Advanced and Less Developed Countries.* Baltimore: Johns Hopkins University Press.

Portes, A., and M. Lungo (Eds.). (1992a). *Urbanizacion en Centroamerica.* San Jose, Costa Rica: Facultad Latinoamericana de Ciencias Sociales—Flacso.

Portes, A., and M. Lungo (Eds.). (1992b). *Urbanizacion en el Caribe.* San Jose, Costa Rica: Facultad Latinoamericana de Ciencias Sociales—Flacso.

Portes, Alejandro, and Min Zhou. (1992). "Gaining the Upper Hand: Economic Mobility among Immigrant and Domestic Minorities." *Ethnic and Racial Studies, 15* (October), 492–522.

Portes, A., and S. Sassen-Koob. (1987). "Making It Underground: Comparative Material on the Informal Sector in Western Market Economies." *American Journal of Sociology, 93,* 30–61.

Portes, Alejandro, and Alex Stepick. (1993). *City on the Edge: The Transformation of Miami.* Berkeley: University of California Press.

Powell, Walter. (1990). "Neither Market nor Hierarchy: Network Forms of Organization." In Barry M. Straw and Larry L. Cummings (Eds.), *Research in Organizational Behavior.* Greenwich, CT: JAI Press.

Prader, T. (Ed.). (1992). *Moderne Sklaven: Asyl und Migrationspolitik in Osterreich.* Vienna: Promedia.

PREALC. (1982). *Mercado de Trabajo en Cifras: 1950–1980.* Santiago de Chile: International Labour Office.

PREALC. (1987). "Ajuste y Deuda Social: Un Enfoque Estructural." Santiago de Chile: International Labour Office.

Preteceille, E. (1986). "Collective Consumption, Urban Segregation, and Social Classes." *Environment and Planning D: Society and Space, 4,* 145–154.

Prigge, Walter. (1991). "Zweite Moderne: Modernisierung und Stadtische Kultur in Frankfurt." In Frank-Olaf Brauerhoch (Ed.), *Frankfurt am Main: Stadt, Soziologie und Kultur* (pp. 97–105). Frankfurt: Vervuert.

Pugliese, E. (1983). "Aspetti dell' Economia Informale a Napoli." *Inchiesta, 13* (59–60, January–June), 89–97.

Queiroz Ribeiro, Luis Cesar de. (1990). "Restructuring in Large Brazilian Cities: The Center/Periphery Model in Question." Research Institute of Urban and Regional Planning, Federal University of Rio de Janeiro.

Rakatansky, M. (1992). "Spatial Narratives." In J. Whiteman, J. Kipnis, and R. Burdett (Eds.), *Strategies in Architectural Thinking* (pp. 198–221). Chicago: Chicago Institute for Architecture and Urbanism, and Cambridge, MA: MIT Press.

Ramirez, Nelson, Isidor Santana, Francisco de Moya, and Pablo Tactuk. (1988). *Republica Dominicana: Poblacion y Desarrollo 1950–1985.* San Jose, Costa Rica: Centro Latinoamericano de Demografia (CELADE).

RECLUS. (1989). *Les Villes Europeennes.* Rapport pour la DATAR. Paris: RECLUS.

Reich, Robert B. (1991). *The Work of Nations: Preparing Ourselves for 21st Century Capitalism.* New York: Knopf.

Renooy, P. H. (1984). *Twilight Economy: A Survey of the Informal Economy in the Netherlands.* Research Report, Faculty of Economic Sciences, University of Amsterdam.

Rimmer, P. J. (1986). "Japan's World Cities: Tokyo, Osaka, Nagoya or Tokaido Megalopolis?" *Development and Change, 17* (1), 121–158.

Rimmer, P. J. (1988). "Japanese Construction and the Australian States: Another Round of Interstate Rivalry." *International Journal of Urban and Regional Research, 12* (3): 404–424.

Roberts, B. (1973). *Organizing Strangers: Poor Families in Guatemala City.* Austin: University of Texas Press.

Roberts, B. (1976). *Cities of Peasants*. London: Edward Arnold.

Roberts, Susan. (Forthcoming). "Fictitious Capital, Fictitious Spaces? The Geography of Off-shore Financial Flows." In S. Corbridge, R. Martin, and N. Thrift (Eds.), *Money, Power and Space*.

Rodriguez, Nestor P., and J. R. Feagin. (1986). "Urban Specialization in the World System." *Urban Affairs Quarterly, 22* (2), 187–220.

Rolnik, R., L. Kowarck, and N. Somekh (Eds.). (1991). *Sao Paulo Crise e Mudanca*. Sao Paulo: Brasiliense.

Roncayolo, M. (1990). *L'Imaginaire de Marseille*. Marseille: Chambre de Commerce et d'Industrie de Marseille.

Ross, R., and K. Trachte. (1983). "Global Cities and Global Classes: The Peripheralization of Labor in New York City." *Review, 6* (3), 393–431.

Roy, Olivier. (1991). "Ethnicite, Bandes et Communautarisme." *Esprit* (Fevrier), 37–47.

Sanchez, Roberto, and Tito Alegria. (1992). "Las Cuidades de la Frontera Norte." Departamento de Estudios Urbanos y Medio Ambiente, El Colegio de la Frontera Norte, Tijuana, Mexico.

Santoso, Oerip Lestari Djoko. (1992). "The Role of Surakarta Area in the Industrial Transformation and Development of Central Java." *Regional Development Dialogue, 13* (2, Summer), 69–82.

Saskai, Nobuo. (1991). *Tocho: Mo Hitotsu no Seifu* (The Tokyo Metropolitan Government: Another Central Government). Tokyo: Iwanami Shoten.

Sassen, Saskia. (1988). *The Mobility of Labor and Capital: A Study in International Investment and Labor Flow*. New York: Cambridge University Press.

Sassen, Saskia. (1991). *The Global City: New York, London, Tokyo*. Princeton, NJ: Princeton University Press.

Sassen, Saskia. (1993). *Migration Systems*. Working Paper. New York: Russell Sage Foundation.

Sassen-Koob, Saskia. (1980). "Immigrants and Minority Workers in the Organization of the Labor Process." *Journal of Ethnic Studies, 8* (Spring), 1–34.

Sassen-Koob, Saskia. (1982). "Recomposition and Peripheralization at the Core." *Immigration and Change in the International Division of Labor* (pp. 88–100). San Francisco: Synthesis Publications.

Sassen-Koob, Saskia. (1984). "The New Labor Demand in Global Cities." In M. P. Smith (Ed.), *Cities in Transformation* (pp. 139–171). Newbury Park, CA: Sage.

Savich, H. (1988). *Post-Industrial Cities*. Princeton, NJ: Princeton University Press.

Sayer. Andrew, and Richard Walker. (1992). *The New Social Economy: Reworking the Division of Labor*. Cambridge, MA, and Oxford, UK: Blackwell.

Sclar, Elliott D., and Walter Hook. (1993). "The Importance of Cities to the National Economy." In Henry G. Cisneros (Ed.), *Interwoven Destinies: Cities and the Nation*. New York: Norton.

Scott, Allen J. (1988). *Metropolis: From the Division of Labor to Urban Form*. Berkeley: University of California Press.

Scott, Allen J., and Michael Storper (Eds.). (1986). *Production, Work, Territory.* Boston: Allen & Unwin.

Sennett, R. (1990). *The Conscience of the Eye: The Design and Social Life of Cities.* New York: Knopf.

Sheets, R. G., S. Nord, and J. J. Phelps. (1987). *The Impact of Service Industries on Underemployment in Metropolitan Economies.* Lexington, MA: D. C. Heath.

Siebel, W. (1984). *Krisenphanomene der Stadtetwicklung arch + d, 75/76,* 67–70.

Silver, H. (1984). "Regional Shifts, Deindustrialization and Metropolitan Income Inequality." Presented at the Annual Meeting of the American Sociological Association, San Antonio, Texas.

Singelmann, J. (1974). "The Sectoral Transformation of the Labor Force in Seven Industrialized Countries, 1920–1960." Ph.D. dissertation, University of Texas.

Singelmann, J., and H. L. Browning. (1980). "Industrial Transformation and Occupational Change in the U.S., 1960–70." *Social Forces, 59,* 246–264.

Sklair, Leslie. (1985). "Shenzhen: A Chinese 'Development Zone' in Global Perspective." *Development and Change, 16,* 571–602.

Smith, Carol A. (1985). "Theories and Measures of Urban Primacy: A Critique." In M. Timberlake (Ed.), *Urbanization in the World-Economy.* Orlando, FL: Academic Press.

Smith, M. P., and J. R. Feagin. (1987). *The Capitalist City: Global Restructuring and Territorial Development.* London: Sage.

Smith, N., and P. Williams. (1986). *Gentrification of the City.* Boston: Allen & Unwin.

Sonobe, M. (1993). "Spatial Dimension of Social Segregation in Tokyo: Some Remarks in Comparison with London." Paper presented at the meeting of the Global City Project, Social Science Research Council, New York (March 9–11).

Stanback, T. M., Jr., P. J. Bearse, T. J. Noyelle, and R. Karasek. (1981). *Services: The New Economy.* Montclair, NJ: Allenheld, Osmun.

Stanback, T. M., and T. J. Noyelle. (1982). *Cities in Transition: Changing Job Structures in Atlanta, Denver, Buffalo, Phoenix, Columbus (Ohio), Nashville, Charlotte.* Montclair, NJ: Allenheld, Osmun.

Stimson, Robert J. (1993). "Process of Globalisation and Economic Restructuring and the Emergence of a New Space Economy of Cities and Regions in Australia." Presented at the Fourth International Workshop on Technological Change and Urban Form: Productive and Sustainable Cities, Berkeley, CA, April 14–16.

Stopford, John M. (Ed.). (1992). *Directory of Multinationals.* London: Macmillan.

Stren, R. E., and R. R. White. (1989). *African Cities in Crisis: Managing Rapid Urban Growth.* Boulder, CO: Westview Press.

Susser, Ida. (1982). *Norman Street, Poverty and Politics in an Urban Neighborhood.* New York: Oxford University Press.

Teresaka, Akinobu, et al. (1988). "The Transformation of Regional Systems in an Information-Oriented Society." *Geographical Review of Japan, 61* (1), 159–173.

Thomas, Margaret. (1983). "The Leading Euromarket Law Firms in Hong Kong and Singapore." *International Financial Law Review* (June), 4–8.

Thrift, N. (1987). "The Fixers: The Urban Geography of International Commercial Capital." In J. Henderson and M. Castells (Eds.), *Global Restructuring and Territorial Development*. London: Sage.

Timberlake, M. (Ed). (1985). *Urbanization in the World Economy*. Orlando, FL: Academic Press.

Todd, Graham. (1993). "The Political Economy of Urban and Regional Restructuring in Canada: Toronto, Montreal and Vancouver in the Global Economy, 1970–1990." Ph. D. dissertation, Department of Political Science, York University, Toronto, Canada.

Toulouse, Christopher. (1992). "Thatcherism, Class Politics and Urban Development in London. " *Critical Sociology, 18* (1) Spring.

Trejos, J. D. (1991). "Informalidad y Acumulacion en el Area Metropolitana de San Jose, Costa Rica." In J. P. Perez-Sainz and R. Menjivar Larin (Eds.), *Informalidad Urbana en Centroamerica: Entre la Acumulacion y la Subsistencia*. Caracas: Editorial Nueva Socieded.

Tribalat, M., J.-P. Garson, Y. Moulier-Boutang, and R. Silberman. (1991). *Cent Ans D'Immigration: Etrangers D'Hier, Français D'Aujourd'hui*. Paris: Presses Universitaires de France, Institut National d'Etudes Demographiques.

United Nations. (1992). *World Investment Report 1992: Transnational Corporations as Engines of Growth*. New York: United Nations.

United Nations Centre on Transnational Corporations (UNCTC). (1991). *World Investment Report: The Triad in Foreign Direct Investment*. New York: United Nations.

United Nations Centre on Transnational Corporations (UNCTC). (1992). *The Determinants of Foreign Direct Investment: A Survey of the Evidence*. New York: United Nations.

United Nations Conference on Trade and Development (UNCTD), Programme on Transnational Corporations. (1993). *World Investment Report 1993: Transnational Corporations and Integrated International Production*. New York: United Nations.

United States Department of Commerce, Office of the U.S. Trade Representative. (1983). *U.S. National Study on Trade in Services*. Washington, DC: Government Printing Office.

United States Department of Commerce. (1985). *U.S. Direct Investment Abroad: 1982 Benchmark Survey Data*. Washington, DC: Government Printing Office.

United States Department of Commerce. (1992). *U.S. Direct Investment Abroad: 1989 Benchmark Survey, Final Results*. Washington, DC: Government Printing Office.

van den Berg, L., R. Drewett, L. H. Klaassen, A. Rossi, and C. H. T. Vijverberg. (1982). *Urban Europe: A Study of Growth and Decline*. Oxford: Pergamon Press.

Vidal, Sarah, Jean Viard, et al. (1990). *Le Deuxieme Sud, Marseille ou le Present Incertain*. Arles: Editions Actes Sud, Cahiers Pierre-Baptiste.

Vieillard-Baron, Herve. (1991). "Le Risque du Ghetto." *Esprit* (Fevrier), 14–22.

Walter, I. (1989). *Secret Money*. London: Unwin Hyman.

Walters, Pamela Barnhouse. (1985). "Systems of Cities and Urban Primacy: Problems of Definition and Measurement." In M. Timberlake (Ed.), *Urbanization in the World-Economy*. Orlando, FL: Academic Press.

Wentz, Martin (Ed.). (1991). *Stadtplanung in Frankfurt: Wohnen, Arbeiten, Verkehr*. Frankfurt and New York: Campus.

Werth, M., and H. Korner (Eds.). (1991). *Immigration of Citizens from Third Countries into the Southern Member States of the European Community. Social Europe*, supplement 1/91. Luxembourg: Office for Official Publications of the European Communities.

Whiteman, J., J. Kipnis, and R. Burdett. (1992). *Strategies in Architectural Thinking*. Chicago: Chicago Institute for Architecture and Urbanism, and Cambridge, MA: MIT Press.

WIACT (Workers' Information and Action Centre of Toronto). (1993). "Trends in Employee Home Employment." Toronto: WIACT (Mimeo).

Wigley, M. (1992). "Untitled: The Housing of Gender." In Beatriz Colomina (Ed.), *Sexuality and Space* (pp. 327–390). Princeton Papers on Architecture. Princeton, NJ: Princeton Architectural Press.

Wihtol de Wenden, Catherine (Ed.). (1988). *La Citoyenete*. Paris: Edilic, Fondation Diderot.

Willoughby, K. W. (1990). *Technology Choice*. Boulder and San Francisco: Westview Press.

Wilson, W. J. (1987). *The Truly Disadvantaged: The Inner City, the Underclass and Public Policy*. Chicago: University of Chicago Press.

World Bank. (1991). *Urban Policy and Economic Development: An Agenda for the 1990s*. Washington, DC: World Bank.

Yamanaka, Keiko. (1991). "Asian and Latin American Workers in Japan: Should Japan Open the Unskilled Labor Market?" Department of Sociology, Grinnell College, Grinnell, IA.

Zelinksy, Wilbur. (1991). "The Twinning of the World: Sister Cities in Geographic and Historical Perspective." *Annals of the Association of American Geographers, 81* (1), 1–31.

Glossary/Index

A

Acquisitions, increased, 48
Affiliates, outward, major investing countries, 72

B

Balanced urban system an urban system where each city in the urban hierarchy is only moderately larger than the one below it and moderately smaller than the one above it; such systems are characterized by a rank rule city size distribution, often thought to represent a condition of equilibrium, 8, 29, 34
Bank lending, by country, 91
Banking, 54
  assets of companies, by region, 63
  centers, offshore, 3, 18–19, 25–27
  employment, 75
  foreign, 75
  in Miami, 78, 80
  in Sydney, 87
  See also Financial centers
Banks
  multinational, economic internationalization, 3–4
  ranked by assets, 13
  world's largest 100, 22
Bretton Woods agreement, 26, 28

C

Capitalization, 23
Capital mobility, national and transnational, 2–3

Caribbean
  primate urban systems, 29–39
  select cities (map), 30
Case studies
  Miami, 78–82
  Sydney, 85–89
  Toronto, 82–85
Central Business Districts (CBDs), 88
Cities. *See* Edge Cities; Global cities; Port cities, decline
Consumer data, 128–129
Consumer prices, 130–131
Consumption patterns, income, 113–116
Corporate headquarters, producer services, 69, 72, 74
Corporate power, 122–123
Cubans, in Miami, 78–82

D

Defense policy, impact of changing, 43
Deloitte, Haskins and Sells, office distribution, 49
Deregulation of financial markets, 25–27, 37, 47, 54, 86, 91–93
Devalorization, 37. *See also* Valorization
Diversity, 122–123

E

Economic globalization. *See* Globalization, economic
Economic importance indicators, urban, 32–33
Economic inequalities, 5–6

Economic internationalization, 3–4. *See also* Globalization, economic

Economy
informal, 106–107
information, 1–2, 6–7

Edge cities a type of urban agglomeration outside the suburban ring, characterized by significant concentrations of offices and business activities alongside residential areas in peripheral areas that are completely connected to central locations via state-of-the-art telematics, 94

EEC (European Economic Community), 15, 18, 39, 41–43

Employment, 120
data, 128–129
destabilization, 102–103
immigration, 103–105
income distribution, 107–111
in Miami, 81
in Sydney, 86
in Toronto, 83–84
trends, 56, 57–59, 60–61, 65

Euromarkets, 25–27

Europe
balanced urban systems, 39–47
location of top firms, 42
population change, select cities, 41
select cities (map), 40
unemployment, select cities, 104

European Economic Community (EEC), 15, 18, 39, 41–43

Exopole a type of urban agglomeration outside the suburban ring, in peripheral areas, 94. *See also* Edge cities

Export manufacturing, 36–37

Export processing zones areas, mostly in low-wage countries, where firms can set up production facilities for semi-finished goods and be exempted from paying tariffs on the value added when reimported into the country of origin, 3, 18–19

F

FDI. *See* Foreign direct investment

Finance
global cities, 20, 22–24
shift from trade, 9, 11, 14

Financial centers
concentration, 89–93
rise, 4–5
spatial organization, 93–96

Financial companies, assets, 62

Financial credit markets, 15

Financial crisis, 55, 74–76, 96

Financial district, Toronto, 82–85

Financial markets, deregulation, 25–27, 37, 47, 54, 86, 91–93

Foreign assets, nonfinancial transnational corporations, 70–71

Foreign direct investment (FDI), 9, 15, 37, 38, 44, 45, 48, 79, 86–89
shifts in flow, 9, 10–11, 12, 14
stock distribution, 16–17

G

Geography of economic globalization, 10–11

Global cities cities that are strategic sites in the global economy because of their concentration of command functions and high-level producer-service firms oriented to world markets; more generally, cities with high levels of internationalization in their economy and in their broader social structure, 4, 18–24, 50, 120
development, 78–82
formation, 95–96
social impact, 99–106, 116–117

Globalization, economic, 6–7, 53, 119–120, 121–124
balanced urban systems, 29
composition, 11, 14
export processing zones, 18–19
financial centers, 90–93
geography, 10–11
global cities, 18–24

Globalization, economic *(continued)*
  institutional framework, 14–15, 18
  manufacturing centers, decline, 4–5
  offshore banking centers, 18–19,
    25–27
  port cities, decline, 4–5
  primate urban systems, 29–39
  shift from trade to finance, 9
  telecommunications, 1–2
  See also Internationalization, eco-
    nomic

H

Headquarters 3, 19, 53, 67, 68, 69, 72, 74,
    100, 119
  in Melbourne, 86, 87
  in Miami, 78, 79, 80
  of producer services, 69, 72, 74
  in Sydney, 87
  in Tokyo, 105
  in Toronto, 83, 84, 85
Homework, industrial, 24, 106–107, 108,
    112, 116

I

Immigration, 46
  Cuban, in Miami, 78
  and employment, 103–105
  in European cities, 46
  in Japan, 112–113
Income, rate of change, 109
Income distribution
  and education, 111
  in Japan, 111–113
  and manufacturing, 108
  and services, 107–111
Inequalities
  economic, 5–6
  urban, 34, 39
Informalization casualization of, or
  making casual, once formalized
  relations, such as employment
  relations, 106–107
Information economy concept used to
  describe an economic system dominated by industries that produce,

manipulate, and/or transmit information; more narrowly, that sector
  of the economy constituted by such
  industries, notably specialized
  services, 1–2, 6–7
Information industries, 1–2, 65
International property, 6
Internationalization, economic, 3–4. *See
  also* Globalization, economic

L

Latin America, 29–39, 79
  primate urban systems, 29–39
  privatization, 37, 38
  select cities (map), 30

M

Manufacturing decline, 4–5, 18, 54, 55,
    86, 100, 120
  income distribution, 108
  in Japan, 112–113
  producer services, 64–65
Mergers, increased, 48
Miami, case study, 78–82
Multinational corporations, 3–4, 36, 53

N

NAFTA (North American Free Trade
    Agreement), 15, 18
NASDAQ (National Association of
    Securities Dealers Automated
    Quotations), 93
Nation-states, 3–4, 29, 50, 90
National capital mobility, 2–3
Nonfinancial transnational corpora-
    tions, foreign assets, 70–71
North American Free Trade Agreement
    (NAFTA), 15, 18

O

Offshore banking centers banking
  centers that escape many of the
  national and international regulations governing banking transactions; they typically are also tax
  shelters, 3, 18–19, 25–27

Organization of work, 100–103, 105–107, 114–115

Outward affiliates, distribution of, 72

Overvalorization, 37. *See also* Valorization

P

Pax Americana, 27–28

Peripheralization, 120–121

Poor, in United States, 101

Population
    change in select European cities, 41
    decentralization in Caribbean, 36
    growth, urban, 31
    of major cities, 126–127
    urban, 34

Port cities, decline, 4–5, 43

Prices, consumer, 130–131

Primate urban system an urban system where one city, typically the national capital, concentrates a disporportionate share of the population and of economic activities, 8, 29–39, 34–36

Processing zones, export, 3, 18–19

Producer services, 55, 76, 122
    complexes, 65–76
    corporate headquarters, 69, 72, 74
    defined, 55–56 employment, 56–61, 65
    export, 61–62 growth, 56–61
    manufacturing, 64–65
    in Miami, 81
    national, 62–64
    production process, 66–67
    in Sydney, 86
    transnational corporations, 68–69
    See also Specialized services

Property, international, 6

Q

Quality-of-life information, 132–133

R

Real estate, 6
    crisis, 55, 96
    in Miami, 81–82
    in Sydney, 86–89
    in Toronto, 82–83

Regionalism, 121

S

Securities firms, largest, 23

Securitization, 18, 26, 92

Services, 100
    growth, 14
    income distribution, 107–111

Services, producer. *See* Producer services

Services, specialized. *See* Specialized services

Sociological studies, 7–8

Specialized services, 9, 37, 43, 47–50, 51, 53–55, 105, 119, 122
    global cities, 19–20
    growth, 5
    in Miami, 78–79
    See also Producer services

Stock exchanges, market size, 24

Stock markets, 37, 47, 55, 75–76, 90–91, 93
    global cities, 22–23
    Sydney, 87

Suburbanization, 36

Sydney, case study, 85–89

T

Tax havens, 27

Telecommunications, 9, 119–120
    economic globalization, 2
    global cities, 19
    in Miami, 79, 80

Telematics telecommunications and computer technologies that allow for instantaneous transmission of information over short and long distances, 2, 6–7

TNCs. *See* Transnational corporations

Toronto, case study, 82–85

Tourism, 36–37, 43
  in Miami, 81
  in Sydney, 86, 88

Trade, shift from, to finance, 9, 11, 14

Transnational capital mobility, 2–3

Transnational corporations (TNCs), 15, 18, 20, 21, 24, 47–48, 55
  growth, 14
  nonfinancial, foreign assets, 70–71
  producer services, 68–69
  ratios, 73
  See also Multinational corporations

Transnational urban system an urban system constituted by cities in different countries that are increasingly linked through the internationalization of economic transactions, particularly in services and finance, 29, 47–51

U

Unemployment, in select European cities, 104

Unionization, 101

Urban economic importance indicators, 32–33

Urban growth patterns by country, 35

Urban inequality, 34, 39

Urban populations, 31, 34

Urban systems
  balanced, 8, 29, 34
  primate, 8, 29–39
  transnational, 29, 47–51

V

Valorization/overvalorization/ devalorization the socially embedded dynamic whereby value (prices, salaries, profit rates) is attached to activities, goods, labor power, firms, or industrial sectors; under certain conditions the value attached can be seen as excessive (for example, the price of land in midtown Manhattan in the mid-1980s) or insufficient (for example, the wages of garment workers in Manhattan at that time), given recent historical trends or the customary relative levels, 37, 54

W

Wages, change, 110

Work, organization, 100–103, 105–107, 114–115

World map, 136

World War II, 28, 44, 86, 101